United States Railroad Policy

Uncle Sam at the Throttle

United States Railroad Policy

Uncle Sam at the Throttle

Jeffrey Orenstein

Kent State University

Nelson-Hall *nh* Chicago

Editor: Dorothy Anderson
Designer: Claudia von Hendricks
Cover Designers: Claudia von Hendricks, Richard Meade
Typesetter: Boston Linotype Composition Co.
Manufacturer: BookCrafters, Inc.
Cover Art: *Balconies* by Connie Vepstas. Photocollage.

LIBRARY OF CONGRESS CATALOGING-IN-PUBLICATION DATA

Orenstein, Jeffrey R.
    United States railroad policy : Uncle Sam at the throttle /
Jeffrey Orenstein.
        p.   cm.
    Bibliography: p.
    Includes index.
    ISBN 0-8304-1205-0
    1. Railroads and state—United States.   I. Title.
HE2757.O73   1989
385′.068—dc20   89-35585
                                                                 CIP

Manufactured in the United States of America

10   9   8   7   6   5   4   3   2   1

Contents

Preface

THE CRITICAL READER IS ENTITLED to know that this book is written by a normative political theorist who wishes to both explain and evaluate contemporary U.S. public policy toward American railroads. As such, it not only respects empirical economics and policy analysis, it also includes important aspects of them within these pages. Nevertheless, this is not a work of original empirical research findings in political economy. Rather, it is an analytical study with (I hope) justified arguments in normative political economy. It examines the ends and means of politics and government and generalizes about them as an aid to understanding and assessing public policy, that is, what government does and what it ought to do. Consequently, it is principally macroanalytical. It draws as much from other scholars' surveys and synthesizing approaches as it does from specialized monographs.

This book is based on several premises. If the author has accomplished his goal, objectivity has been maintained, because these premises do not color the analysis. Whether a set of facts or premises makes an author happy or not, he or she has a scholarly obligation to describe, explain, and predict as the facts at hand dictate, not according to whim or prejudice. Instead, these premises (or, as some call them, biases) hopefully contribute to an informed choice of problems analyzed and a perspective on what the assembled facts mean.

The first premise is simple: rail transportation is important. Even in the space age, its technology is vital. Railroads ought to be included prominently in the U.S. transportation mix and policies because they have a high social utility with a relatively low social cost. This is not to deny the importance or value of other transportation modes — rather, to emphasize that railroads are worthy of perpetuation.

The second premise is a bit more complex. As a political scientist interested in normative political theory and policy analysis from the perspective of political economy, I believe that different choices and perspectives yield outcomes with significant policy differences for society and the quality of life. Therefore, examining political economies and policies (the kinds of political and economic systems we have and their characteristic policy outcomes) is a good analytical approach, especially for government involvement in railroading, a subject that contains both economic and political components.

A good political scientist (or economist, or other social scientist) is also engaged in scholarship, making judgments (with evidence for them displayed so that others may make up their own minds on the meaning of the data) and attempting to suggest reasonable conclusions. While there is ample need for those who study facts alone, my choice is to study both facts and premises or values and theorize upon them, in the tradition of normative economists and political scientists from Thucydides to Walter Heller.

I might be termed a "practical capitalist." Capitalism makes sense to me both as a set of working facts and a set of moral values. A *practical* capitalist is still a capitalist, but one without a slavish ideological marriage to capitalism or any other social instrument. Capitalism, like all political economies, should be looked at as a means to a better life for the largest possible number of citizens, not as an end in itself. For that reason, I am willing to embrace a mixed economy, with government involvement in certain areas when it is clearly required as a means toward that better life. Government and public enterprise are no more ends than are private economic activities. Each is a useful instrument with appropriate tasks in a good political economy.

No detailed knowledge of railroading or transportation theory is presumed or needed for these pages to make sense, for I have defined conceptual approaches and key terms as the context demands. Similarly, only a general knowledge of the economic and political history of the United States and the operation of its political and economic systems is assumed. A few key details will also be sketched in these pages as needed.

Finally, this book is dedicated to those policymakers and railroaders who re-created a viable transportation artery of which the nation can be proud. Now that Conrail is in the private sector, it is well to remember that its value to its stockholders and the nation was largely created by public policy. Its successful quasi-nationalization played a decisive role in the face of tremendous odds. It was a commendable achievement of the American political economy that ought to be understood and evaluated as a potentially viable policy option in the future.

The strengths of such an analytical work are due in large measure to the many talented individuals who assisted in its preparation; its failings are mine. Special thanks are due to Virginia Orenstein for her unfailing good business and accounting judgment, to my colleague Dr. Warren Norton for his critical encouragement and his editing finesse, to Joan Manahan and Darla Dunn-Waldrop of the Stark Campus for their assistance in the preparation of the manuscript, and to the offices of Ohio Congressmen Howard Metzenbaum, John Seiberling, Ralph Regula, and James Traficant. A great debt is also owed to those many Conrail and Amtrak people in Ohio, Washington, and Philadelphia who took time out from running a railroad to talk at length to an inquisitive professor who asked about the railroad instead of the trains. I also wish to thank those on the Kent State University faculty who contributed their knowledge and resources in many ways. Without them, this work would surely be less than it is.

chapter one

Public Railroading in a Private System

HIS IS A STUDY OF GOVERNMENT POLICY toward railroads in the United States. It focuses on the present and the near future, but it cannot — and does not — ignore the past.

Railroads and the federal government have matured together in the United States. The first spadeful of earth for the first steam-drawn common carrier railroad in America was turned in 1828 by a signer of the Declaration of Independence.[1] Since that time, the government and railroads have continually cooperated and fought, but have remained interlocked.[2] It is impossible to study the history of either without understanding this interaction.

What characterizes the past and present of American railroading more than anything else is the presence of Uncle Sam at the throttle in this free enterprise economy.[3] Even though the United States has a lively free enterprise tradition, direct and indirect government participation in the economy takes place.[4] In the transportation field, especially, it started with the earliest road and canal building efforts, continued during the creation of the Interstate Commerce Commission in the nineteenth century, and intensified with the temporary nationalization of railroads during World War I, the government promotions for emerging transportation modes, and the rail quasi-nationalizations of the present era. Railroads, particularly, have been major targets of both direct and indirect interventionist public transportation policies for over a century and a half.[5]

In the 1970s and 1980s, this tradition of public policy continued, albeit with a change of course. Direct government intervention and the regulatory reform movement sweeping through the corridors of government increased Uncle Sam's power in American railroading.[6] Whether that change is a temporary aberration or a permanent factor in American public rail policy remains to be seen. What is certain is that Uncle Sam's role has changed both in direction and scope in the recent past.

By the early 1970s, America's railroads were in a deepening crisis. The healthiest of the privately owned railroads, those in the western part of the United States, suffered from rates of return on investment alarmingly below the costs of capital. They also faced declining business and were forced to interchange business with the deteriorating rail systems of the Midwest and, especially, the Northeast. Passenger service had virtually collapsed.

A century and a half of national public policy on transportation produced a legacy of subsidies to railroad competitors and an uneven, seemingly alternating policy of support and punitive regulation for American railroads.[7] The Penn Central Railroad and six other eastern lines were in the depths of bankruptcy and physical deterioration, which threatened a densely populated, politically connected, and heavily industrialized section of the nation with virtual collapse of essential rail freight and passenger services. Something had to be done, and the private sector of American railroading was seemingly without the capacity and/or the will to act effectively. The public, shippers, and the press called for quick solutions. The stage was set for government intervention, just as it had been on the eve of World War I. In most political and economic systems, such a crisis would have led to sweeping nationalization of the railroads on the basis of their being a public utility that must be maintained at any cost. But in the United States, increased federal involvement with the rail transportation system was relatively limited and, in the case of Conrail, transitory.[8] And, from the limited perspective afforded by closeness in time to the situation, it was largely successful.

The creation of Amtrak and then Conrail, the privatization of Conrail, the "statelization"[9] of many short freight railroads and commuter passenger services, and the sweeping changes in the regulatory climate have contributed to a new (and still evolving) era of public railroad policy.[10] It is a reluctant Uncle Sam, however, who peers out of the locomotive down the public policy track ahead, searching for signals. Political and economic events have put him in the cab of the locomotive, but the culture and traditions of the U.S. political economy and the trend toward pro-private enterprise policies that characterized the Reagan years warn him that he ought to get off at the earliest safe and convenient station.

A brief review of events illustrates this point. On April 1, 1976, the political economy of the United States was altered by a major direct government intervention into the private economic sector. It was the birth of a new railroad created and 85 percent owned by the government, the Consolidated Rail Corporation or Conrail. The new government railroad was an unavoidable congressional response to the bankruptcy of the Penn-Central and other railroads that had threatened to seriously disrupt, possibly even halt, essential rail service to much of the industrial heartland of the United States.[11]

On its first official day of operation, the Consolidated Rail Corporation was like any other new public policy: merely a promise by the public sector to do something in the face of public demand and need. In this case, the promise was that the U.S. government would build a profitable and reliable railroad from the rail crisis. Just over a decade later, on the eve of Conrail's privatization, the promise was fulfilled. Conrail was making a handsome profit and running reliable rail service, and had become an important actor in the political economy of the United States. That kind of turnaround is noteworthy for any railroad, much less a quasi-nationalized one that did not fit the normal models of either a private business or a government agency.[12]

Amtrak, the National Railroad Passenger Corporation, underwent a different evolution.[13] It had been formed in 1970 by the government as a way of preserving a core system of rail passenger service in the face of huge passenger-service deficits incurred by private railroads and a flood of petitions to permanently abandon trains to the Interstate Commerce Commission, the regulatory agency that had the authority to determine the fate of each passenger train run by a common carrier. By the time of Conrail's birth, Amtrak was six years old and losing large amounts of money while providing only fair service. It owned no tracks, and operated trains on the tracks and with the crews of private railroads known to be unsympathetic to passenger service. Eventually, Amtrak followed Conrail down the path of quasi-nationalization, after detours down the paths of private and more fully nationalized corporate organizations. It has settled into being a virtually permanent government corporation, as I shall detail in later chapters.

A third major event was the 1980 enactment of the Staggers Rail Act.[14] This landmark statute ended almost a century of the federal government's efforts to closely regulate the railroads' economic activities and "deregulated" both public and private railroads to a significant degree. It essentially allowed railroads to set their own rates and service levels according to the transportation marketplace. While maintaining some limited economic regulation and keeping safety regulation intact, the Staggers Act allowed railroads to compete on a more equitable basis with other modes of transportation as well as with each other. To date it has succeeded, with both service and railroad profits holding above pre-1980 levels and haulage rates on key commodities like coal actually declining.[15]

By 1987, the Staggers Act had proven effective, even though electrical utilities urged Congress to reconsider it.[16] Private railroads were in better physical and fiscal shape than they had been for decades, in spite of years of tough times for most of their major industrial customers. Conrail had become profitable by 1981[17] — a state-of-the-art railroad that provided excellent service.

Even Amtrak's fortunes improved somewhat. It acquired its own railroad right of way for an important portion of its routes, and its service levels dramatically improved systemwide in both perception and reality. Ridership increased. The earlier trial balloons to defund and/or sell Amtrak floated by the Reagan administration failed, and the operating ratio (expenses to revenues) continued to improve, although it was not approaching profitable levels.[18]

On March 26, 1987, however, it was not business as usual for Conrail. Uncle Sam's railroad had reached the end of the line as a public entity. On that day, the federal government got out of the rail freight-hauling business by selling all of its 58.8 million shares of the Consolidated Rail Corporation in one massive privatization move. This more than $2 billion New York Stock Exchange sale was the largest offering of a new equity in U.S. history.[19] It represented the government's 85 percent interest in the now-successful corporation it had formed by legislation only eleven years earlier. So popular was the equity in this unprecedented privatization that not only was all of the stock sold the morning of the first day's trading, but the aftermarket had driven up the government-set initial price of $28 per share to $31.875 before the closing bell. The stock held between $30 and $40 until the general crash of October 19, 1987. And even then, it fell less proportionally than the Dow-Jones Average and climbed back by late 1988.

Methods and Scope of Analysis

Analysts inevitably raise many questions about public policy, and federal rail policy is no exception. For example, what framework(s) of analysis do we use to make sense of complex phenomena? What is there in the U.S. political and economic systems that makes the United States different from other Western industrial democracies with nationalized railroads? What role should the U.S. government play in rail transportation? What made the federal government change its policy on Conrail but not on Amtrak, Staggers, and other railroad policies? Why did the government get into the railroad business in the 1970s? Did the recent intervention differ from the nationalization of the railroads during World War I? Was it the same kind of government ownership and operation of railroads that is common in other Western industrialized democracies as well as avowedly socialist countries? Were American railroads "broke," and should the federal government have tried to "fix" them? Was the fix that was applied the best possible policy? What will be the future of public policies on American railroading? What ought it to be? What is likely to happen to these railroads, public and private, in the near future? What should we (and others) learn from Uncle Sam's experiences at the throttle?

These and other questions about the federal government's involvement in railroading are the subject of this book. It attempts to explore these fundamental questions about the political economy of American railroading and Uncle Sam's role at its throttle. If it is successful, it will examine these questions within the broad theoretical framework of public policy analysis grounded in political economy and place them in the context of American history and political culture.

Let us begin with the observation that complex events of political and economic policy do not just happen. They are legacies of past ideologies, institutional arrangements, and policy choices, modified by what can be called "luck" or variable social forces.[20] But even if these events are complex, they are understandable by a process of orderly investigation and conceptualization. A sound analytical approach should place complex public policies in their "real" context. Since that context cuts across normal academic boundaries, our inquiry should follow reality. It attempts to do so by drawing upon insights and methods from many appropriate fields. Thus, this study relies heavily upon political science (especially political theory and public policy),[21] and borrows from economics (especially normative economics and political economy),[22] transportation,[23] history,[24] and even sociology.

Policies and events make their mark in the workaday world of political economy. They have tangible legacies in specific policies like deregulation and institutions like the Consolidated Rail Corporation (Conrail) and the National Rail Passenger Corporation (Amtrak). These institutions provide services that are vital to the nation and, therefore, are in the public interest; they are not just abstractions. To the extent we understand them, we are in a better position to make them work. However we might feel about it, the federal government is likely to play a permanent role in rail transportation. A viable transportation system is necessary if the nation wishes to remain a great industrial power.

This work relies heavily on description and analysis of these public policy legacies. It employs what are called, for lack of a better term, extended case briefs. These are shorter than a book-length case study but longer and more detailed than an example or skeletal summary. They are interwoven with text throughout the book rather than placed in separate chapters. The case briefs look at Conrail, especially, and Amtrak in a moderately detailed and contextual manner because these are the most important contemporary legacies of the American political economy of railroading and because they show the range of probabilities for government involvement in railroading. Other examples are developed in less detail as appropriate.

The history of these legacies, their major characteristics, their problems and prospects, their effectiveness, and their competing alternatives play an important role in this analysis. But it should be understood that these case-briefs do not exist in a vacuum. They can be understood best through the application of sound analytical theories. While there are many valid theoretical approaches to understanding public policies like these, with significant economic externalities, the conceptual approaches called *political economy* and *public policy analysis* seem most appropriate for a variety of reasons. We can combine them into a general conceptual framework that allows us to examine simultaneously the economic and political components always present in the public policy of transportation in a manner that can give us a basis for sorting out the economic and political components, seeing how they interact, and allowing comparison and contrast with different transportation policy regimes.

The definitions of political economy and policy analysis are relatively straightforward. It is only their application that can get complicated as we delve into enormously complex and murky social problems. According to economist Edmund Phelps, "Economics arose in response to questions of political interest about the national economy...[and] its vitality and development continue to stem from this central concern.[25] Thus, "the main subject in political economy [is] the *choice* of economic systems and public laws and policies that society has available for coordinating and rewarding its members' participation in the economy."[26] Phelps quotes a letter to William Temple written by the eminent British economist John Maynard Keynes when he brings out another aspect of political economy: "[E]conomics, more properly called political economy, is on the side of ethics. . . . There are practically no issues of policy . . . which do not involve ethical considerations."[27]

In other words, economics concerns not only public policy but also making sound normative judgments.

A definition of public policy as a subject and conceptual approach is just as straightforward and remarkably similar. Herson puts it this way: "In simplest terms, public policy is what government does and does not do. Public policy is contained in the laws, judicial decisions, and administrative rulings that determine the benefits and constraints that come from government. An inquiry into public policy not only looks at the benefits and constraints, but it also looks to see which groups are helped or hurt by those benefits and constraints."[28]

Nagel puts it similarly. He defines public policy as "governmental decisions designed to deal with various social problems,"[29] and he describes public policy analysis as "the determination of which of various alternative policies, decisions, or means are best for achieving a given set of goals in light of the relations between the alternative policies and goals."[30] Public policy is what the public sector does about the major social problems of the day, many of which are predominantly economic and virtually all of which have important economic components.

Both economics and political science, then, are different ways of viewing the interfaces of the political and economic sectors. While economics as conceived by Keynes concentrates on the economic sector of society and recognizes spillover into the political sector, public policy analysis concentrates on the political sector and recognizes spillover into the economic sector. Thus, an integrated approach of political economy makes sense. As Phelps puts it, "Political economy is not the same as political science. . . . Yet, inevitably, the explanation of the reward structure by reference to the *effects* of society's chosen economic institutions and policies shed some light on the *causes* of those institutions and policies."[31]

Good public policy analysis and good political economy inevitably lead to prescription. They both make informed choices about what should be done — what paths are best and why — as suggested by the data and the assumptions of the analysts. The two approaches are quite properly normative, because it is insufficient for an applied analysis to merely explain what happens. Phelps writes: "But just as it would be strange to have physics without engineering or biology without medicine, political economy has a second, more practical side.... *Normative* political economy studies the structure of rewards (and accompanying institutions) *as they would be* if the society introduced different economic institutions or government policies. . . . Normative political economy *criticizes* the prevailing reward structure and underlying economic mechanisms. . . . It [and empirical political economy] is quite scientific. Both involve the constructing of theoretical models."[32]

This applies to public policy analysis as well. Because society is the legacy of struggles to provide a decent life for society's members, through institutional construction and policy decisions, it does not follow that it is perfect and unchangeable. What has been done in good faith frequently becomes obsolete or dysfunctional and needs to be changed after careful analysis in order to accomplish the original goals in changed environments. Thus, normative political and economic theory are parts of a long history of people trying to cope with public affairs and make sense of their institutions and technologies. The case of governmental involvement in contemporary American railroading is rooted in that tradition.

This chapter has raised some general issues and provided definitions. Chapter two focuses in more detail on the political economy of railroading. It delves further into political economy in general, examines the specific parameters of the American political economy, then turns to the nature of rail transportation and its interrelationship with the political and economic cultures of the United States.

Chapter three moves into the extended case briefs. It looks at the history of the American political economy of railroading and isolates the roles and legacies of public policies, especially government regulation of railroads from the beginnings of that technology to the present. It looks at the choices made (and the choices not made) in the political economy. Then, using those choices, it turns to Conrail and Amtrak (and less explicitly public and/or less enduring railroad institutions and issues) and compares them and contrasts them with past choices and with other models and issues already developed in the analysis.

The second part of this book focuses on the normative aspects of rail public policy and is both descriptive and predictive. Chapter four examines the policy options of the political economy of U.S. railroading in the present and the near future. The final chapter, the most normative of all, assesses the lessons we ought to learn from deregulation, quasi-nationalization, and other public policies in contemporary American railroading. The chapter concludes with prescriptions about the role the government (and other legitimate actors) should play in the political economy of U.S. rail transportation for the remainder of this century. It links the ideas raised in this chapter with the descriptions and prescriptions in the remainder of the work. No claim is made for the absolute validity of these ideas. They are offered in the spirit of a contribution to a long and vital discourse in political economy and political theory.

Railroads are vital to the present and future of the United States. Even though we have not nurtured railroads as a matter of public policy to the extent that industrialized nations in Europe and Asia have, railroading is a critical American industry and will remain so. Though trucking is firmly established on a subsidized highway network, U.S. industry moves about one-third of its raw materials and finished products by rail. Also, the only efficient, long-range solution to the growing problem of large-scale, short- and medium-distance people-moving in an urbanized nation is rail transport.

Rail technology can and should be supplemented by other transportation technologies, but it cannot be replaced by them. Therefore, the political economy of the United States for the rest of this century and into the first quarter of the next cannot be separated from its railroads. Obviously, something that important cannot escape the attention of government as well as private enterprise. That attention should be studied and evaluated so that we are in a better position to make the right choices.

chapter two

The Political Economy
of American Railroading

THE PREVIOUS CHAPTER INTRODUCED the concepts of political economy, public policy, and government involvement in American railroading. This chapter expands upon these foci to paint a theoretical mural of the political economy of railroading in the United States.

Political Economy

Phelps writes, "We can safely say [that] political economy . . . is a long-running debate over the mechanisms of competitive markets . . . in which consumers have to buy their goods but can shop around for offers and enterprises compete for consumers with quality and price. It is a debate over *Economic liberalism* started by Adam Smith. . . . The critics of this liberalism declare that real-life markets are grotesquely *in*efficient, in part because they are (unavoidably) not very competitive either. . . . The political economist is largely engaged in clarifying and weighing the pros and cons of markets, regulated or unregulated, as devices for the operation of the economy"[1] (Phelps' emphasis).

Political economy is a body of knowledge about alternative economic and political systems. On a broad methodological level, it is a framework that encompasses both the polity and the economy. As a result, its typical applications to policy

11

analysis combine insights and approaches from both political science and economics, and even sociology and psychology, in explications of complex social phenomena. Political economy allows us to make the important observation that most political activities focus upon and regulate economic subjects just as most economic activities impact upon (and often attempt to authoritatively allocate) social and political goods for society.[2] It is useful to view these phenomena in a framework that integrates the normally separate political and economic levels of analysis. Other researchers have shown the way by adopting this sweeping perspective.[3]

As applied in this book, political economy is not a developed theory (in the scientific denotation of that term) that stands ready to generate quantitative data. (A quantitative study of public policy toward railroading might examine the same phenomena using analogous approaches and evaluate aspects of policy performance statistically.) Rather, it serves as a comprehensive vehicle to assess the public policies of government involvement with railroads in the United States and to grasp something about its characteristics and limits.

Our approach also allows us to use political economy prescriptively to generate a comparative analytical framework about alternative levels of public and private allocation of values.[4] This, in turn, allows us to apply broad socio-political values (political theories or ideologies, depending upon the specifics)[5] to these institutions and gives us a probabilistic framework for moral evaluations. It allows us to make statements such as, "If private enterprise is good, then something that denies it is bad."

The best way to define political economy in this context is operationally, that is, by breaking it down into its political and economic components and then recombining them. Logic dictates that we need to view each preliminarily so that we have data to compare and contrast as we form an integrated approach, both theoretically and operationally. Politics and economics both involve public relationships of people. Each is characterized by the interdependence of strangers who are forced to deal with each other directly or indirectly in order to survive as neighbors on the same small planet. Global wars, economic depressions, or oil boycotts affect the scarce resources and material relationships and institutions of this planet and thus involve all of its citizens politically and economically.

Politics and Government

Politics and government have a rich history that extends back to ancient Athens and earlier. Though the writings on these topics span two-and-a-half millennia and contain innumerable disagreements about the precise meanings of politics and government, certain themes recur often enough to serve as a basis for definition of these concepts.

Politics (at least for most political theorists) has a broader reach than economics, encompassing public decisions that have economic targets and many that do not. It involves public interactions of people who share the same territory and time (as opposed to distinctly private or individual activities which affect only a few, usually those who directly consent to them). It is a broad (but not limitless) set of relationships concerned with public integration. It involves conflict and consensus about who gets what, when, and how.[6] It is about who (if anyone) is elected, the quality of our environment, who regulates our public utilities, and many similar topics.

Politics is the process by which we come to terms with others who share our society and, often, our institutions. There is no prescribed method of having or doing political relationships. They can be peaceful or not so peaceful, rational or not so rational. While not strictly defined by governmental structures or policies, or the values we pursue in our public relationships, politics surely involves them all eventually. Thus, it includes crucial and often contentious decisions about economic allocations, including how to run a railroad.[7]

Government is easier to understand because it is more limited than politics. It is the way we organize and regularize our political relationships; it is their institutionalization. Government is shared by citizens and used to make and enforce rules and rights for society. It is also a tool to allocate those public goods and services that are necessary for a decent life, including transportation.

Governments can be simple or complex, good or evil,

coercive or liberating, efficient or inefficient. They can be engines of destruction or agencies of conflict resolution. They can be a means toward cost-effective, responsive, and just political relationships, though this outcome is never guaranteed.[8]

In order to insure that such potentially abusive institutions remain just, it is helpful to recall the classical liberal notion in political theory that governments have no absolute justification. To the extent that they deserve our taxes and support and the right to legitimately regulate our railroads, they must earn it. They merit support (what political theorists call political obligation) and are valid targets of our demands as long as they provide society with an effective vehicle for securing the public interest.

The notion of instrumental justification of government has its roots in Western political and economic thought. According to the mainstream of Western democratic and egalitarian traditions,[9] governments must do what they are supposed to do (and are suited to do because of their impartiality and vast resources) or they do not merit our support. They might even merit our opposition if their failures are serious enough.

The ancient Hebrews, the classical Greeks (including the political economist Aristotle), and, more recently, Rousseau, Hobbes, Locke, Mill, Green, Keynes, and others (not including the political economist Marx, who was hostile to government and expected the community to perform its integrative and allocational functions) have contributed to a discourse that defines the purpose of institutionalized political communities. This discourse justifies inherently coercive and costly governments only because they are useful. They can (and must be made to) provide the structures, processes, and policies that create fair, abundant, and satisfying public relationships between individuals. The discourse pictures a society in which individuals contract their economic and political rights to a government as a matter of convenience, but still maintain those rights and can revoke them if necessary. The liberal discourse justifies the state and its client institutions, like Amtrak and Conrail, because they are in the public interest or it does not justify them at all. It rejects conservative or organic theory conceptions, which justify the state absolutely as a creature of natural law, irrespective of what the state does.

This defense and limitation of the state leads to what may be called the political theory of public utilities. Arising from the center of both classical and post-classical liberalism, it is a major aspect of the foundation of the political economy approaches commonly pursued in the non-Marxist industrialized world. It is even creeping into some Marxist revisionist approaches to political economy as openness and restructuring become part of the Soviet Union's current vocabulary of political economy.

It starts with the individual and his or her rights and needs for what Hobbes called a "commodious life" and develops a set of basic public needs or utilities that each must have in order to survive and develop, if not flourish. In effect, it "operational-izes" the public interest and provides a tool for analyzing what government should or should not be doing politically or economically.

Neither societies nor social analysts have achieved universal agreement about what ought to constitute the public interest and government's role in it. Disagreement forms the heart of the limited ideological clashes that characterize current Western political economies, separating the Tories from the Laborites as much as the "liberal" Democrats from the "conservative" Republicans.[10] Even so, these ideological combatants have similar lists of necessary public utilities. The agreement of both free-market and social reform liberals on such governmental goals defines liberalism and generally limits clashes to means rather than ends — to the appropriateness of their public or private provision.

The Western individualistic tradition suggests that the legitimate needs of the majority are the same as the legitimate functions of the state and constitute a basic agenda for the state. The tradition simultaneously develops a standard of measure for reasonable and unreasonable state actions (figur-ing prominently in theories of revolt as well as private enter-prise) and outlines the bulk of the public interest; the provision of basic, useful, and vitally necessary services for the population.

While the list of what fits legitimately under such a category of public utility is controversial and constantly changing according to ideology and technology, certain basic categories appear frequently. A typical list usually rejects luxuries, private needs which apply to only a few, and exploitative needs of individuals, because they overtax scarce resources, are best pursued privately, or are socially intolerable. National defense, energy, education, public safety protection, communications, and transportation of people and goods are found on most lists. Western liberalism has assigned to the state a central role in providing these needs directly or in regulating and encouraging private interests to provide them under license.

As this classical theory of public utilities was accepted in the West, it served as justification for many functions of the state, and the importance of transportation to the theory became easily discernible. European and North American governments developed road networks, waterways, and railways (and later, air and highway networks) either under public auspices or under public control for political and economic development reasons. In some government systems, this led to permanent government ownership of transportation infrastructures. In the United States, a mixture of occasional, often temporary public ownership and varying degrees of regulation of "private" transportation firms has become the pattern.

Transportation was quickly recognized by developing Western governments as necessary for expansion and maintenance of a growing state and economy. Private firms operating without government protection and resources (and control) were generally thought not to have sufficient incentive or perspective to allocate this public good in the public interest. That Western tradition of transportation as a public utility helps to explain why Conrail and Amtrak were created in a system that normally eschews government enterprise. When private enterprise fails, basic transportation needs remain part of government's obligation to provide a network of public interest infrastructures.

This conceptualization of public utilities underlies the justification of nationalization or quasi-nationalization of public utilities by some liberals and the regulation of utility delivery by loosely regulated private firms by other liberals. It assigns special functions to legitimate governments and argues that they are the only agencies in modern, complex societies that have two necessary characteristics for the just provision of public utilities, whether directly or indirectly. First, government is the only institution in society that possesses the enormous resources to set up or regulate comprehensive networks for vital services like defense, energy, and transportation. Second, government ought to represent all citizens equally and therefore is obliged to respond to the elementary interests of all, not merely those with sufficient financial resources to have a significant impact on the economy. Thus, political equality should foster economic equality, at least in satisfying basic needs in an affordable manner.

A connection exists between Western political theory and public policy. In Herson's words, "[the] *politics of ideas* refer[s] to the strategies and arguments that result in one idea (or set of ideas) coming to a position of dominance in political life. Thus, the politics of ideas is the struggle to shape the future of public policy — thereby shaping the future of political life."[11] In current Western society, the dominant politics of ideas demands that public policy create a political economy (not necessarily limited to a government) that satisfies a basic set of needs for all as the first priority. Efficiency and equity are frequently applied criteria; they will be used throughout this book.[12]

Economy and Business

The economic component in political economy is also the heir of a long and venerable tradition of Western thought and debate. John Maynard Keynes, Karl Marx, and Adam Smith are contributors to the mainstream of Western economic thought, as are Albert Camus, John Locke, and Jean Jacques Rousseau. Economic institutions like Conrail and Amtrak can be understood only through an understanding of the institution of business and its role in a given political economy.

Business may be defined as the institutionalization of a broad set of material relationships and values called an economy. A business firm is an organized institution with its own rules, roles, structural patterns, and moral justifications, which are formed and guided by the economy's relationships and values. The business institutionalizes economic goals by producing goods and services and making them available to the public.

In an essentially capitalistic system like the United States, however, business firms have the additional role of profit center. They are supposed to sell a product or service for more money than it costs to make or provide it; the excess money is considered legitimately earned (as long as it is not "excessive" or a "windfall") and at the disposal of the owners of the firm. While there are other claimed roles (like public service and social allocation) for firms in a capitalistic economy, any business operating within a free enterprise system must consider its profits to be primary if it is to survive over time. Pursuit of these other roles (externalities) is usually forced by government regulation [13] or tax incentives.

Profitability is important not only to strictly capitalistic firms but also to quasi-nationalized ones. Amtrak no less than Norfolk Southern is judged by its bottom line: the more profitable, the better it is judged to be by the culture and the government and the more it is likely to succeed.

Musselman and Hughes define economics as "a science that deals with the satisfaction of human wants through the use of scarce resources of production."[14] They look at the economy as a set of materially oriented relationships between people in a society with legitimate purposes and functions (specifically, to allow human beings to relate and come to terms with each other in their dealings with valued production, goods, and services). Like political systems, economies are not merely abstract sets of relationships. Through the politics of ideas — history, tradition, culture, institutional coercion, and the like — they have acquired goals. In economies like those in North America, these goals are generally deemed to include promoting growth, encouraging price stability, promoting a rising standard of living, maintaining full employment, providing equitable distribution of income, ensuring economic freedom, and providing financial security throughout the whole economy.[15]

All economies value similar goals (except freedom, perhaps), and they all contain some type of institution (not necessarily business firms as we know them in the West) designed to allocate these values and institutionalize these goals. Those values and goals enumerated above are explicitly capitalistic; other economies differ more in degree and emphasis than in kind.

To understand what business firms do and why, keep in mind that the goals of a political economy are system goals, not those of individual firms. Businesses wish only to sell a product or service in order to maximize profit or meet assigned national quotas and are content to allow the society and the government to set and attain other socio-economic goals.

Although many business firms and economists point to the social benefits of business enterprises,[16] there is sufficient evidence to conclude that, in practice, these benefits (however real they may be) are accidental and/or secondary to profits or quotas. Even when social goals are pursued, they are seen as ways to maximize profit by improving the image of the firm. Firms within an economy are in business to provide a return on investment for their stockholders or to satisfy bureaucrats, not to satisfy public opinion or public policy, unless they must.

Business firms must do what the society allows and expects of them or be without rationale. They are socially valuable as institutions in a larger entity only and are obligated to pursue the values that that entity provides for them. If they cannot do so, they are usually transformed into government agencies (if their functions are deemed indispensable) or are allowed to disappear.

Politics and Economy Recombined

We are now in a position to draw a few generalizations about the concept of political economy. It is generally agreed by both politicians and business practitioners (as well as political scientists and economists) that the primary function of government in a political economy is to act as an agent of the general public interest. This agent is entrusted by society to allocate goods and services and to set material and other policies for the people.

In the postindustrial West, however, governments gradually have given away much of this allocatory responsibility and right. Currently, private or semi-private firms that are government owned but virtually free to do what they like[17] often act together in a market to provide public necessities like transportation. Such firms influence and even dominate whole sectors of the economy and even the government itself, since they have the power to block unfavorable legislation and lobby for favorable legislation and regulation. Clearly, this situation exists at the pleasure of an ideology and society that wants it to exist and that maintains the power to change it. (We will examine this more closely in the section following on the American political economy.) The economy and its business institutions differ from the polity and its governmental institutions in one critical respect. The economy does not have an overall institutionalized regulator of the public interest except for the imperfect operations of the market or the narrow interests of key firms within it. There is no institutional analogue of the government except as society has allowed.

Musolf writes, "The institutions that best symbolize the clash between the respective mind-sets of government and business, it seems to me, are the handful of government-sponsored enterprises that official documents describe as private and profitseeking."[18] Material relationships essentially operate in a vacuum, subject only to the forces of the marketplace or potential governmental regulation. These relationships are an important area of politics and political economy. Most economic decisions are made by governments or given over by governments to markets or individual firms in free enterprise societies.

To summarize so far, legitimate politics and government constitute only one aspect of the framework of political economy. The economy, business firms within it, and their purposes and functions are all critical components. Together, they constitute the operational context of political economy as an environment for government intervention into the operation of railroads. Tabb's comment in relation to ghettos can be applied to transportation:

> Political economy . . . is the tradition of those who think of economics as the study of men in their roles as producers and consumers in a social setting. Thus . . . [an object of a case study in it] is studied as an economic unit of a larger society.[19]

This leaves us impaled on the horns of a dilemma. We recognize that business and government are analogous in many respects. Yet, they have conflicts and different outlooks on goals as well as means. Luckily, political economy allows us to extricate ourselves from this dilemma by giving us a framework for integration.

The politics of ideas have supplied governments with the task of defining and securing the public interest. This is not done altruistically, in spite of self-congratulatory rhetoric by politicians. Governments do so because they must. They are rewarded if they are successful and punished if they fail. Democratic governments earn re-election and the all-important popular legitimacy that taps a deeper dimension of political culture than the public opinions of the moment. Nondemocratic governments pursue popular legitimacy so that they may continue to exercise their authority without fear of rebellion.

On the other hand, we have seen that profits and the satisfaction of bureaucratic mandates through the sale of products or services are the major operational goals of firms. If these goals can be reached through stock trading, takeovers, mergers, or other non-sales sources, so be it. The allocatory benefits of the missing production do not concern the firm. Its managers are selected by stockholders or administrators to maximize return on investment because this is the aim of private institutions. The general goals of the economy (full employment, equity, a favorable balance of trade, energy independence, etc.) are not their responsibility, no matter how large the firm. That falls to government under this political economy of ideas.

As a result, in many political economies, business operates in the public economic sector with goals and authorities appropriate to the private sector, and we have governments with the responsibility and authority for the economy operating largely outside of the economy. In other words, governments customarily allocate the society's economic goals, while businesses directly operationalize the goals according to their own self-interest.

Governments and businesses also differ on the means by which to pursue their goals. Governments ultimately use authority. They rely upon citizen compliance with laws, taxes, and business regulations. Successful ones do not use terror, but elicit popular sentiments of legitimacy by fulfilling the popular will. This, of course, is backed by the threat (and occasional use) of force and some subtle massaging of public opinion through propaganda and symbol manipulation.[20]

Business firms pursue their goals by cost-effective production and aggressive marketing in a usually competitive marketplace. They earn their profits or bureaucratic rewards by beating competitors at their own game, or appearing to do so. If this is insufficient, they may use fraud, shoddy products, or manipulation of regulation to get their way, in the manner of governments in a similar bind.

The differing goals and means of business and government culminate in the two having different traditions. In a liberal political economy like that of the United States, government sees itself as an arbitrator and intervenor for justice in the economy, the inheritor of a long tradition of intervention into what business does. Business sees itself as a just, reasonable allocator of goods and services dispensed through contract between corporation and consumer, with government having only the role of "night watchman" in the process. In effect, the politics of ideas have evolved into a governmental tradition of social-welfare liberalism, while business's tradition is one of laissez-faire liberalism.

These general differences in outlook and culture manifest themselves most frequently and obviously in politicians' popular rhetoric and political campaigns. But they also direct behavior and organization of both business and government to an intangible but important degree. Because these major differences on ends, means, and traditions exist, strategies for resolving them in the day-to-day realm of politics and the economy are numerous in the history of our nation.

Business and government are not permanent, irreconcilable adversaries that exist like weights on a jeweler's balance scale — one's ascendance proportionately depressing the other. Tension between the two can be resolved in a variety of ways. Either can be ascendant at the expense of the other; they can be roughly balanced with moderate ascendancy of both; or either can gain hegemony but not complete dominance. As Phelps alluded to in his definition of political economy, any given point of balance between them may demarcate a type of political economy, or at least a sub-type. Thus the various strategies for resolution of public and private sector differences are the major defining characteristics of political economies. How societies provide public services like transportation is resolved ultimately in general public policy. In this regard, transportation is not analytically different than defense, criminal justice, energy, or any other vital public utility. Ultimately, it is not a question of whether public allocations of public utilities are going to be made, but whether they are made in the public interest and by public, private, or mixed providers.

When viewing political economies historically and comparatively, a continuum of possible types emerges. It contains four major political economies: "pure" allocation and regulation by the market; market allocation enhanced by government; quasi-nationalization; and nationalization. Each has been used with varying degrees of success to provide utilities for societies, and each is a general rather than a closed category. Each is properly conceived of as a demarcation of a political economy.

Market allocation lies at one side of the continuum. It allows individual producers and sellers to interact in a way that sets prices and determines supplies of goods and services, and generally allows an "invisible hand" (as conceived of by the classical economists) to allocate and regulate both public utilities and luxuries for the society.[21] It does so without any intervention by public authority, save for the provision of a basic infrastructure of economic exchange, contract enforcement, and so on.[22]

In the words of Galbraith, "The market, let me remind you, is the regulatory apparatus that takes the place of state authority.... And to be an effective regulator, the market must be an impersonal force beyond manipulation by any individual or organization . . . so there is nothing any one buyer or seller can do to influence the market."[23]

The pure market as an allocator must be so intensely competitive that the entry or exit of any individual producer or buyer does not affect it. A truly free market is also not affected (except perhaps by the maintenance of conditions for its existence) by the policies or budgetary might of any government. No one person or institution sets prices or policy in a pure market. Oligopoly,[24] or the presence of but a few buyers or sellers, is not conducive to a market economy. A few producers tend to act like a single producer by definitively setting policy and/or prices and thereby denying the competition that drives the market.

It is assumed that the pure market impersonally controls what consumers and firms do through a social network of regulation created by the market itself. By reward or lack of it, the market political economy controls prices, service levels, technological advancement, efficiency, and so on of goods like transportation. It allocates these values for the society. It is an article of faith among market advocates that this allocation is accomplished in a socially satisfying and effective manner over time, causing needs to be fulfilled and opportunities and challenges to be available for the courageous.[25]

These assumptions are accurate to a point because they work in practice for certain commodities like grain or for elementary services like haulage of goods on one's back. Everybody's grain or back resembles everybody else's, and none can dominate. Pure competition therefore exists. For most of the material exchanges in complex industrial societies, however, such a truly free market is more of an ideal than a reality. There are either too few sellers or too few buyers for true competiton and/ or insufficient incentives present in the market to allocate the public interest effectively.

In industrialized transportation especially, pure markets seldom, if ever, exist, as even a cursory overview of transportation costs and spatial economic activities and location theory suggests. The many nonmarket variables, such as subsidies and natural marketing areas, that Sampson, Farris, and Shrock[26] and most other transportation analysts[27] describe, make a convincing case that capital-intensive and high-technology transportation services resemble natural monopolies or oligopolies far more than pure markets.

Some services, like police or fire protection and most rail passenger transportation, are needed by the society but cannot be allocated efficiently by the market because of sporadic use or because individual buyers cannot afford to pay for the true cost of providing the service. The social benefits (saving lives, energy and land-use conservation, and so on) of the products or services are too remote to the individual consumer to be visible to or deemed worthy of sacrifice by individuals. Yet, they are necessary. It usually falls to governments or their allocatory agents to purchase or subsidize those products with the resources of and for the benefit of the collectivity. This is a major problem for pure market political economies and often a reason why they are opposed and replaced.

Their usual replacement is not a major departure from the old system, however, but "simply" a market economy enhanced by government actions. Located adjacent to the pure market on our continuum, such a political economy maintains the market as the dominant allocator of goods and services. However, it uses government to guide, nudge, and cushion the effects of a pure market according to the moral goals of the political theory of public utilities.[28] The government, as an agent of the greatest good for the greatest number, influences the economy through tools that fall far short of direct government business ownership. This lets individual producers and buyers do what they will according to market incentives, but sets the tone of these incentives and guides the producers and buyers toward the public interest.

The most common public intervention in markets in recent American transportation history (due to the economics of scale necessary for providing modern transportation) has been antitrust regulation. Such regulation limits the size and expansion of dominant firms in a given industry[29] so that competition is preserved.

Frequently, the political economy of government-enhanced transporation markets also regulates a large range of other economic behaviors. Governments sometimes set minimum or maximum prices, mandate services, and require equity in pricing for all customers regardless of costs involved. They also mandate economic spin-offs of social regulations (requiring noise suppression devices on locomotives in order to make the world a quieter place to live, for example), incentives for desirable behavior (tax credits, land grants), and many similar business and individual behaviors.

In all of these interventions, public agencies set the goals of the marketplace as official policy goals and manipulate the individual actors within to make certain that those goals are met for the economy as a whole. Thus, in theory, the market is not transcended but enhanced. In practice, of course, poor judgments and obsolescence can negate the social value of some of these enhancements. Business firms and customers respond to the incentives and disincentives of a market and still retain vast areas of freedom, but the market is modified and limited in the name of the public interest.

A government-enhanced market political economy is still largely a market political economy. Private firms and individual consumer decisions allocate most values and services. Government attempts to act as an equilibrium-producer to keep things running justly. In the industrialized world, especially the United States, this is a common ideology of transportation and political economy.[30] While it does not model the United States, Canadian, or most Western European political economies exactly (most are more interventionist and try to regulate on more, often contradictory, fronts), it is the liberal ideal upon which they are based and the standard of measure by which they are frequently evaluated. The degree of government enhancement in such a system varies widely over time and among cultures. Nevertheless, it is analytically separate from either a pure market economy or an economy with more direct government participation.

However well-intended they are, detailed economic regulations become obsolete and tend to distort markets as well as to enhance them if they are not carefully conceived and regularly monitored.[31] The record of governments is a poor one here. Because of these problems, societies often try to make regulatory practice consistent with ideology, as the deregulatory movement has aimed for in the United States.[32] Failing that, they turn to other forms of political economy. One of the least understood and increasingly common ones is the political economy characterized by significant quasi-nationalization, involving partial and indirect government participation in actual provision of goods and services. Quasi-nationalization is a hybrid allocation of economic values and goods, integrating the public and private sectors. It is a shift toward the direct public provision side of our continuum.

In an otherwise-government-enhanced system, quasi-nationalization[33] of major firms in important sectors of the political economy embraces elements of both nationalization and regulatory enhancement of markets. It differs from each, in degree rather than kind. In spite of laissez-faire cultural reluctance to even flirt with nationalization, quasi-nationalization is an emerging form of political economy that has embraced the Consolidated Rail Corporation and the National Railroad Passenger Corporation in the United States at various times in their corporate history and is commonplace in Europe and Canada. Musolf says, "Mixed enterprises occupy a political and economic no man's land in the United States, though they are regarded as unexceptional, even commonplace, in many parts of the world. The relatively great vigor of U.S. private enterprise ... helps make public-private joint ventures appear rather anomalous in the U.S."[34]

Quasi-nationalized firms differ from nationalized ones. They are designed with the management practices, organizational patterns, and external economic and political relationships characteristic of privately held firms in free-enterprise political economies. These include profit expectations and management financial incentives for success. They are expected by their founding governments to regulate their political economies by example and deed in the marketplace. These firms are supposed to be cost-competitive, while operating under equal regulatory and market constraints, and to be socially responsible by maintaining necessary services and thereby force their private competitors into social responsibility and efficiency.

Governments develop and finance these firms (or acquire them from their previous private owners) and stand prepared to dig into their deep pockets to cover unprofitable operations via direct subsidy. Governments often are also prepared to reap any profits these firms earn, although the Reagan administration chose not to do this and privatized a profitable Conrail instead.

In this sense, the government functions as a well-endowed stockholder who has confidence in management and does not usually interfere with their prerogatives as long as profits are earned. Such firms resemble their private competitors operationally. Standing at trackside, the railroad or business expert would not have been able to discern any relevant differences between a preprivatization Conrail and the CSX Corporation. Only an accountant would have seen the differences in Conrail's sources of last-resort capital and ownership and would have found them irrelevant once the railroad earned a profit.

In common practice, most liberal governments in such de facto if not de jure political economies do not embrace quasi-nationalization because of a desire to improve the social milieu. Such transformations are usually reluctant, last-ditch attempts to save failing enterprises with great public utility. Governments facing crisis are forced to put aside their conservatism and enter economic sectors where private firms are absent or failing because "the resources required were too large, the risks too great, or the likelihood of profit too small to attract private enterprise."[35] Musolf[36] argues that these quasi-nationalized firms are usually organized on a for-profit basis (at least as a goal) from the outset because of the prevailing free-enterprise cultural norms that constrain policymakers' perceptions.[37] The hope is that they are but temporary expedients and there will be a return to other, more market-oriented forms of political economy when conditions warrant. This is what motivated the Reagan administration's successful drive to privatize a profitable Conrail. A quasi-nationalized political economy deviates from a nationalized one in that the firms within it usually have fewer social mandates. They are not expected to be employers of last resort, providers of hopelessly uneconomic services, or cross-subsidizers for other politically well-connected beneficiaries of public policy. Competition in the marketplace with other private firms and the need for profits usually preclude government from requiring such mandates.

In reality, such a political economy substantially resembles more orthodox capitalistic political economies. Inefficient or unlucky private firms of similar social importance that fail under private ownership are customarily afforded similar advantages under bankruptcy policies. This has been common with railroads in the United States, for example.[38] Failing firms are given breathing room to reorganize on a more profitable basis, are often given governmental financial aid (loan guarantees), are excused from many of their already limited social mandates, and are protected from their creditors. Though this is not an entitlement (as witnessed by the liquidation of the Chicago, Rock Island, and Pacific Railroad),[39] it is common enough to support this hypothesis.

In the final analysis, quasi-nationalized political economies differ only incrementally from government-enhanced market and more fully nationalized political economies. What is more, they resemble the former more than the latter. Whether by default or design, they exist (especially in North America) and might evolve into valid twentieth century innovations in the practice and discourse of political economy.

The state socialist[40] or nationalized political economy encompasses extensive direct government participation in the economy to the virtual exclusion of private enterprise and markets. In doing so, this last pole of political economy on the continuum departs the realm of classical liberal economic and political theory occupied by the other political economies, though it grew from the same roots. It is characterized by direct government participation in the production of goods and services through state development, ownership, and operation of the means and factors of production in pursuit of the public interest, as inspired by the ideas of Marx and later revisionists.[41] Wholesale pursuit of profits and competition with private enterprise are normally eschewed in socialist variations of this practice, although limited private enterprise is occasionally tolerated for its motivational effects on workers. Fully socialized systems should not be confused with the so-called full welfare states of Europe and elsewhere.[42] Although characterized by significant nationalization, the politics of ideas in these welfare states encourages private enterprise. Thus, they are not fully socialistic and belong somewhere between quasi-nationalization and full nationalization, even though the individual nationalized firms resemble their socialist analogues.

Fully nationalized firms are typically owned and operated in a manner similar to government departments. They have government-appointed boards of directors and must meet central economic and political planning goals. Revenue-enhancement and efficiency are desirable but not mandatory. These firms are also customarily mandated to provide a wide range of social services that are only tangentially linked to their principal economic tasks. Undoubtedly, this limits their profitability. This is also why they receive widespread political support on the part of policymakers and users alike.

Thus, railroad, business, and accounting experts watching the Soviet State Railways, the British Railways, or the Swiss Federal Railroads servicing a remote hamlet with state-of-the-art, lightly patronized passenger trains would observe that these nationalized entities behave quite differently than pre-privatized Conrail. They act more governmental in a de facto as well as a de jure sense.

Full nationalization has some advantages. The resources of a whole nation can be mobilized quickly in a national emergency like war. When well-run, nationalized firms can provide very good, technologically advanced products and services to the consumer, often without incurring large deficits. They make it easier for policymakers to directly accomplish goals such as economic development of depressed areas and environmental protection. They also serve as deterrents to the few exploiting the many in the name of unregulated free enterprise.

Nevertheless, there are disadvantages associated with nationalization. Some argue that nationalized political economies lack accountability through the market and therefore are less efficient than their private analogues.[43] Though actual efficiency records of nationalized political economies are mixed[44] (some do well and others do poorly, just as with private firms), this is a charge that must be taken seriously. As the Chinese have discovered under the regime of Deng Shiao-Ping, fully nationalized political economies have two other potential drawbacks. They can stifle incentive, thereby lowering productivity, research, and development, contributing to lack of international competitiveness, and they have a disturbing tendency to fail to integrate national planning goals with local enterprise capabilities effectively because of the massive bureaucratic environment associated with them.

In conclusion, though the advantages of nationalization (efficient mobilization of resources, good service, and excellent technological research and development) are worthy of pursuit, their long-term costs are very high. Luckily, many of the policy goals of nationalized political economies can be reached in less regimented forms of political economy at the lesser cost of an indirect regulatory bureaucracy with unpredictable impact. While no political economy is perfect or universal, those ranging near the center of our continuum seem to produce greater benefits with fewer costs.

Consequently, more and more economically developed governments (those fortunate enough to possess the resources to allow freedom and diversity in spite of their inefficiencies) are attempting to avoid the extremes in political economies.

Quasi-nationalized political economies and government-enhanced market systems, or ad hoc combinations of the two, have become the norm in the industrialized countries today, with the notable exception of the Soviet Union and some of its client states. Even there, however, policymakers like Gorbachev seem to be doubting the wisdom of their present political economies.[45] Though both orthodox Marxists and laissez-faire ideologues dislike the present trends, the middle ranges of political economies appear to be the dominant trend for the present and the near future.

The American Political Economy

The political economy of the United States fits into the middle ranges of our continuum, as it is mainly a government-enhanced market. But U.S. politics and economics have many unique characteristics.

First of all, the U.S. political culture is characterized by a blurring of economic and political policy institutions, in spite of a laissez-faire policy of limited government. As Asch and Senaca put it, "We have placed a very substantial portion of our economic decisions in the public sector, and we have kept them there despite our own complaints."[46] Another characteristic of the American political economy is a political culture dominated by "classical" liberalism. In Dolbeare's words, "The dominant system of thought in American political life ... sees the individual as a rational, self-interested person, entitled by nature to certain "rights" such as life, liberty and property."[47] U.S. economic culture is dominated by liberalism as well. Classical liberal notions of private property, free enterprise, and individual liberty thoroughly dominate our views on material relationships. Again, in Dolbeare's words, "An important unstated assumption is that private striving to fulfill needs provides the 'best' means ... of distributing economic and other rewards of social life."[48]

Another characteristic of the U.S. political economy is its institutional complexity and variety. Public policy-making is diffused and therefore difficult to control by policymakers and policy subjects alike, although their voices are involved in its formulation. Musolf characterized it in this way:

> The complex background of private-for-profits [quasi-national-ized corporations] is matched by the intricacies of political decision-making on the U.S. scene. Separation of powers, disunited political parties, numerous strong interest groups, localism among elected representatives — these and other political features are associated with the rampant pluralism characteristic of policy-making in the United States. The wide variety of [economic] organizations on the margins of the state is a product of not only the vitality of U.S. society, economy, and political life, but of the concomitant reluctance of policymakers to impose order on this chaotic way of fashioning public policy.[49]

Finally, U.S. political economy is characterized by a tension between authorities and jurisdictions in both the public and private sectors. The system has no effective, ongoing, central-ized economic planning. It relies on an enhanced market for its direction and is reluctant to stray far from its classical liberal roots and techniques. It continues to employ publicly regulated private allocations of goods and services (letting transportation supply and operating firms dominate U.S. transportation planning and legislation, for example) and only occasionally launches into quasi-nationalization when a crisis occurs. Again, Dolbeare sums it up as follows: "Americans continue to use rhetoric about individualism and the dangers of government action while employing government on an ad hoc, pragmatic basis to do what seems necessary at the moment to alleviate suffering and promote specific goals."[50]

Politics

No political system can be understood without knowledge of its political culture, a set of first principles of political life. Herson writes that the political culture

> may be taken to mean the do's and don'ts of political life. In less simple terms, a political culture is variously defined as a widely shared set of values concerning government and politics, a widely shared set of understandings as to what government

ought to do and ... the purpose of public policy.... [It] helps shape the politics of ideas in at least two ways: first by narrowing the alternatives that will be seriously considered in the resolution of issues; and second, by contributing to the processes in which political issues are formed.[51]

The notion of political culture is a helpful analytical device, an effective way of ordering perceptions about the world which abstracts the political ideas (including much of what is customarily categorized as economic) and analyzes them. These political ideas[52] set the tone for society's important ideals, institutions, and policies. Ultimately, they control them. Just as a giant skyscraper's visible superstructure rests upon invisible foundations, so do the visible institutions and policies of the political economy rest upon the foundations of political culture. Those wishing to understand or, more ambitiously, to modify public policies must do it through the political culture or suffer frustrations.

While the many analysts of U.S. political culture differ in details, they all agree that the culture is dominated by liberalism. Hartz[53] describes the United States as a classical liberal society without the extremes of political and economic ideas characteristic of European polities. In his view, the original English middle-class settlers in America (given the dismissal of Native Americans) brought only their classical liberalism with them. Since there was no feudal side of the political spectrum, no socialist revolutionary tradition grew up to oppose it. That left the settlers with a society of the middle, with liberals and conservatives agreeing on liberal ends and arguing on means. Thus, there was a cultural "tyranny of the majority." This was observed by the nineteenth century French conservative visitor to America, Alexis de Tocqueville,[54] who felt that policymakers and citizens were bound by this cultural ethos.

Hartz argues that this kind of political culture was bound to be capitalistic, because captalism favors those with resources and entrepreneurial abilities rather than those with traditional title and few resources, for example, those who dominated the formative events in this new political culture. Furthermore, he claims, this kind of capitalistic political culture was bound to be at least nominally democratic, because democracy (especially

when coupled with de facto restriction on meaningful participation of all but the rich) favors the ability of citizens to exercise
their resources equally in pursuit of personally advantageous
public policies. Those with superior resources, therefore, are not
threatened by a political decision-making structure that allows
all to use what powers they have in establishing public policy.

Hartz believes that the American political economy was
characterized from its beginning by the almost total institutionalization of the political culture of laissez-faire liberalism and
diffuse, quasi-democratic institutions, backed up by the elite
vetoes inherent in a separation-of-powers system. He sees the
pursuit of individual liberty to be the primary American value,
taking precedence over equality or other values. Other analysts
disagree with him, at least in degree. Gunnar Myrdal (in the
style of Thomas Jefferson) sees an American political creed, not
necessarily behavior, that is characterized by the dignity of all
and the belief that people have inalienable rights of equality
and liberty.[55] Similar sentiments have been voiced by Parrington, and Boorstin, and others.[56]

In modern political science, the political culture is frequently
looked at as being more complex. Herson, for example, develops
an American cultural inventory that includes liberty in both its
negative (freedom from) and positive (freedom to pursue goals)
forms, but also incorporates equality, achievement, justice,
precedent, the rule of law, localism, and the most fundamental
American value of all (in his view), representative democracy.[57]
Eisinger, Dresang, Fowler, Grossman, Loomis, and Merelman
have a similar catalogue that also includes nativism and
emphasizes the tension between governors and governees and
the role of democracy in resolving it.[58]

The institutional mechanisms of the American political
system form the political component of the American political
economy. These institutional mechanisms are liberal because
many of the same individuals who dominated the formation of
the American political culture also dominated the institutions.
Liberal elites wrote, or influenced the writers of, the Declaration
of Independence, the Articles of Confederation, the U.S.
Constitution (and its early amendments and judicial interpreta-
tions), and the early legislation and court decisions that built
U.S. political structures. These structures are extremely com-

plex.[59] They are characterized by the presence of both federalism and separation of powers. Federalism here refers to the overlapping and division of sovereignty and authority of two or more governments operating in the same territory; it manifests itself in the United States in over 86,000 governments, many of them internally divided, functioning under a system of separation of powers.[60] Federalism is a legacy of the thirteen separate British colonies of colonial America, none of which wanted to give up their own institutional separateness. It was enhanced by the influx of immigrants who often wanted their own space and institutions in the new nation. A contributing factor was the massive decentralization that inevitably resulted from westward expansion across the continent before modern transportation and communications allowed cultural and political integration.

Perpetuated today, federalism creates many overlapping and often conflicting jurisdictions with legislative, regulatory, taxing, and judicial authorities. It can serve to breed innovation and progress in public administration, but it often does not. Instead, with alarming frequency, it breeds conflicting standards of public policy and administration which prove economically and politically costly and inefficient. Federalism also allows special interests with locally overwhelming resources to divide and conquer state and local governments; we can observe this when a major industrial concern starts a national site location search for a new facility.

The other distinctive institutional characteristic of the American political system is separation of powers. This grew out of the founding fathers' deep-seated belief that because people are morally flawed, they cannot be trusted to keep the peace so must be divided and restrained for their own good to prevent "a state of war of all against all," in Hobbes' words.[61] Led by Madison,[62] they built a complicated series of interlocking governmental components, each with different constituencies, different requirements for action, and overlapping terms and social compositions. These components included an independent and indirectly elected chief executive with veto power, a bicameral legislature (with different terms of office, apportionment requirements, and selection procedures, at least before senators were popularly elected), an independent and appointed-for-life judiciary (which seized the power of judicial review after *Marbury v. Madison* in 1803), elections staggered in time and scope, and so on.

The system requires various branches of government to check and balance each other as they make policy. It was built upon the theory that tyranny (probably of that most feared faction of all, the unpropertied majority, if Madison is correct in Federalist No. 10) could be prevented if the same people did not make and enforce the laws and policies of the political system. It was not foreseen that this system allows dominant interests to capture just the major portion of one component and thereby hold government action hostage to their demands. Also unforeseen by the founding fathers is that, in peaceful, calm times, the shared liberal political culture of economic and political elites would cause the different branches of government to have similar outlooks and thus preclude the checking functions of separation of powers. In times of great ideological polarization like the Civil War, however, the system deadlocked and could not solve pressing problems through politics. The founders also failed to perceive that while democracy is the most effective controller of tyranny known to political theorists and constitution builders,[63] a separation of powers system diffuses public opinion and frustrates popular control of government.

Separation of powers was mimicked by most of the emerging 86,000 governments in the federal system, yielding a staggering institutional complexity by the time railroads developed. This made the U.S. political economy inefficient and conservative, as well as creating the conditions for its capture by well-organized interests.

If national policies need concurrent majorities in the House of Representatives, the Senate, the White House, and the federal courts, a majority of any one of them (even one key individual in certain circumstances, such as a committee chairman, a federal judge, or a president) can block the will of a strong majority in and out of government. When extraordinary majorities come into play, the situation is magnified. When Congress is attempting to override a presidential veto or ratify a treaty, a key individual or a minority of 34 senators and the president can frustrate the policy goals of all 510 other congressmen and Supreme Court justices, for example. In this way, special interests (operating through well-financed political action committees and public relations consultants) and demagogues who are attractive to the news media have many points of access into the system. It is far easier to establish a working hold on one critical component of a separation of powers system than to influence a simple majority of governors, as in a parliamentary system without judicial review.

Hence, legislation and regulation detrimental to those interests able to capture a critical piece of the system is often deflected. Unless public opinion exerts great pressure to break the logjam, special interests may dominate the policy process. In practice, the public is not usually so involved. The result is the blurring of policy directions and an unpredictable route for legislative, administrative, or judicial policy initiatives.

Finally, this must be superimposed upon the political culture's conservative legalism and emphasis on precedent, "the belief that established legal means and regular procedures are the only proper way to resolve issues,"[64] and the tendency for an issue's resolution by this complex, imperfect process to remain in force until compelling interests use their access to the policy process to change them. Together, these are the institutional characteristics of the American political system.

The complex apparatus of American political interactions and interests has relevant implications. It encourages minority control, as we have seen. But because it allows so many different and powerful participants into the process, it creates a fertile ground for delays and abrupt changes of policy direction, policy inconsistencies, and incompleteness. It is also inefficient in resource allocation; therefore effective planning is virtually precluded, leading to "the crisis of public authority" that Lowi talks about when he critiques American pluralism.[65]

The changes in regulatory direction of American railroads illustrate the point. Inconsistent regulatory policies (moving first to encourage railroad development, then to regulate railroads, then to encourage them again in the 1920s, then to deregulate them recently) allowed a few U.S. railroads (mostly those in the West, with access to land-grant-era natural resources, lower costs, and higher revenues due to geography) to prosper in a changing, heavily regulated environment. Most railroads languished and declined, earning very poor rates of return on investment for most of this century. Their struggle to cope with the changing policies and institutional intricacies of the American political system led not only to bankruptcies and federal involvement with railroads, but also to lowered efficiency and greater consumer costs. Changes in regulatory direction have also played a major role in preventing implementation of a more rational national transportation system, as outlined in the final chapter.

Economics

Similar cultural and institutional dynamics operate in the American economic system. It is safe to say that the American economic ideology includes the same liberalism and the same debates about the public versus the private interest we saw in relation to political subjects. Just as with classical political liberalism, "its social base was initially the rising seventeenth-century middle class.... The liberalism of the dominant middle-class merchants and financiers reigned virtually unchallenged.... Non-liberal arguments...were either ignored or repressed as un-American."[66]

These middle-class Americans used their concepts of freedom and natural economic rights to argue the case for extensive property rights for all, regardless of the problems involved when individuals with unequal resources compete with each other in an unfettered market. This laissez-faire cultural ethic differed in emphasis from that which stressed more general human rights. Social-reform liberals argued for the extension of rights beyond just those of property (for example, free speech), but they still included property rights in their ideas. All of this economic thought was solidly rooted within the liberal tradition, and it still influences the contemporary political economy.

As Dolbeare and Hartz have claimed, the range of debate effectively excluded American conservatism[67] and radicalism as mainstream, policy-initiating philosophies, although there have been some loud voices advocating these ideas in American history. Socialism, feudalism, syndicalism, anarchism, and the like have been as absent from mainstream U.S. economics as they have been from mainstream U.S. politics. The effective American economic culture has been confined largely to a dialogue between laissez-faire and social reform liberals.

Herson summarizes this situation effectively when he writes, "Of course, we have known since the earliest days of the republic that ours is both a political system and a political economy, but what we did not discover until the arrival of the positive state was the extent to which the political economy dominates the political system."[68] The economic and the political are not separable in American culture, ideology, and thought. The dialogue between the laissez-faire and the positive freedom streams within U.S. culture characterizes the view of the world shared by the two and maps the cultural dynamics of the American political economy.

On an institutional basis, the American economy is as complex as the American political system. At the governmental institution level, "the president has been given major, but not exclusive, responsibility for directing the economy, but he operates through a bureaucracy that he cannot always control … [with a partially independent civil service in major executive agencies, etc.]. He shares his responsibility, however, with the two chambers of Congress [and the Congressional Budget Office, the General Accounting Office, multiple Congressional committees and subcommittees, etc.] and two independent regulatory commissions: The Securities and Exchange Commission and the Federal Reserve Board."[69]

On a nongovernmental level, the situation is equally complex. The government shares de facto economic policy-making abilities with a vast array of private and quasi-private institutions. These include important multinational firms, international organizations, various securities exchanges, the foreign and domestic investment communities (particularly, large institutional investors who can provoke changes with their massive leverage), important economic interest groups like trade associations and organized labor, academic and private economists, and so on. These groups compete with each other and with the governmental institutions for control of the direction of the American political economy.

In effect, the cumulative power of these nongovernmental economic institutions constitutes a form of public power clothed in private garb by those who stand to benefit from federal economic policies. The permissive institutional complexity allows private economic institutions to allocate resources for the whole economy in spite of separation of powers and other constitutional impediments to factional control.

Thus, even when its own directions are coordinated, the government only indirectly directs the economy. It must work with and through these private policymakers. This gives private policymakers a large share of power to set the economic agenda for the nation, even though no single private power is a consistent winner. The government's taxing, spending, and social-steering programs are "fought for and constructed in the arena of interest-group competition and bargaining ... [making public policy in the economy] a temporary equilibrium between contending factors and forces.[70] In essence, the economy is decentralized and often is incapable of being steered. It is fair to say that the powerful economic interests that gain access to the machinery of the American political system because of its decentralization use that access to secure and maintain the upper hand, in many cases. Rational planning and the public interest are frequent casualties in this process.

Political Economy

When we assemble all of these elements, we have a general picture of the American political economy, a system with intertwined political and economic subsystems. Both components of the political economy are characterized by institutional complexity, significant public and private decentralization in decision making, and a largely shared liberal culture, albeit one with internal tensions on the proper extent of government and private power.

This political economy forms the context for both economic activities and public policy in the United States. It is both a cause and an effect of major issues like government involvement in railroading. Herson writes that "values within the political culture are not confined to government and politics alone. They affect social and economic behavior and they derive from these behaviors as well."[71] These values operate through an economic and political institutional complex that magnifies their congruence and serves to reinforce the clout of the powerful. The U.S. political economy is nondirect and incremental, and serves to keep public and private business going as usual.

Both political and economic structures serve as lenses to focus attention on public problems and produce public policy solutions to them that tend to be liberal and incremental. It is unlikely to be otherwise, given both the lenses and the source of energy beamed through them. As Weaver puts it, "In the United States, for example, the system of checks and balances between the executive, legislative, and judicial branches of the federal government and the fragmentation of power within these branches (notably within Congress) makes it especially difficult to impose losses on well-organized and powerful groups."[72]

Herson sums up the policy output of the American political economy quite effectively when he writes, "[American] nondirect policy is incremental.... It is policy that copes.... It often works at cross purposes with other policies.... It reconciles conflicting values within the political culture. It proceeds from interest group competition."[73]

Herson, Weaver, and other political theorists and economists quoted here point out that the political economy of the United States is based on a powerful, complicated ideology and is composed of a set of institutions. The complexity of the political economy accounts for public and private behavior in relation to the political economy. Railroads and government policies toward them are not exempt.

Transportation and Railroads

Transportation is a deceptively simple concept; however, the radical implications of transportation must be understood by the policy analyst because of its key place in an industrialized political economy. Thus, they bear brief review. Transportation is the purposeful movement of people or goods from point A to point B, the changing of the location of an item.[74] Its political, economic and social significances strongly affect the economic and political development and the life-style of nations or regions.

Transportation can be accomplished by a private shipper, who moves goods strictly as a means to his economic well-being, not as an end in itself. A power plant that moves only its own coal from its mine to its coal pile at its generating site via a dedicated conveyor or private railroad (like the Black Mesa and Lake Powell Railroad in Arizona) is an example. The owner of the coal moves it because he needs it in a certain place, not because there is any intrinsic value or extrinsic social benefit in its transportation. Although this kind of transportation is important to those that do it, it is not very relevant to public policies regulating the whole political economy, because it is a private rather than a public act.

Another kind of transportation is more public and more germane to our analysis. Prevalent in industrial societies are entities called common carriers. These are transportation providers licensed by public authority to provide transportation as a service for hire to others and their goods. They are legally required to provide reliable, nondiscriminatory service to all at reasonable rates.[75] They can be sustained either by collection of user fees, by government subsidies, or both. To the common carrier, transportation is a principal focus, since it brings in critical revenues. To the society, however, it is merely an important public utility.

Regardless of how it is organized, transportation is vital to modern society. Citizens in all societies "are dependent on transportation for economic, social, recreational, educational, cultural, political, and other purposes. Nevertheless, because transportation is a means to an end and not an end in itself, it is often taken for granted," Harper suggests.[76] Because it is taken for granted, transportation often receives less public policy support than its utility would suggest as appropriate.

Transportation is as important as any other single factor in explaining economic and political development. Areas denied access to good transportation, whether for natural or political reasons, fail to develop and prosper. Areas with adequate transportation develop faster and more thoroughly, in spite of other obstacles (in most cases). Early cities and commercial areas were located on bodies of navigable water when that medium provided the best transportation.[77] Later, as technology affected transportation, cities developed along primitive roads and early railroad lines just as surely as urban sprawl followed limited access highways in the automobile age.

Transportation remains a critical catalyst of economic, social, and political development at all stages of political economy. In fact, it virtually defines such stages. When changing technology and a changing climate of political economy caused a relatively rapid shift during the 1950s of passenger travel from the train to the private automobile (and to the airplane, to a much lesser extent), the implications were enormous. Urban areas that had grown around central rail depots soon found themselves with burgeoning suburbs, that demanded more highways, airports, and nontransportation services, and with decaying downtown cores, underused public transportation, and a shrinking tax base to fund needed services. Housing and commerce followed the prevailing mode of transportation swiftly, causing long-term shifts in the political economy.

The life-style of a nation parallels transportation to a great extent. Can the proliferation of fast-food outlets and shopping malls be coincidental or preliminary developments to the spread of highways and private automobiles as major people movers in the United States? While it cannot be "proven," it is logical to conclude that transportation was a major causal factor in their development just as the presence of water was a factor in the location of New Amsterdam, the great cities of the Rhine Valley, or the urban industrialization of the Great Lakes.

Analogous phenomena can be observed in Europe or Japan. There, urban sprawl and automobile-centered life-styles exist, but are less prevalent. Cities are generally more compact and have thriving cores because of the survival of heavily used passenger railroads. This was the result of deliberate public policy and has led to the development of the still growing T.G.V. networks in France, a similar system in Germany, and the "bullet train" in Japan, along with the necessary rail and bus feeder networks that typically center on the railroad station. It should also be noted that these political economies are more centralized institutionally than their counterparts in the United States, allowing less private allocation of public goods and making comprehensive public transportation policy and planning more likely.

The spreading freeway network in Europe may be sowing the seeds of the automobilization of European political economies today. It remains to be seen whether projects like Bahn 2000 (the Swiss policy of making railroads more convenient and even more modern than present) can continue to command the large pro-rail constituency necessary to prevent the widespread automobilization without alternatives that characterizes the United States. Perhaps the greater population density and premium on efficient land use will cause Japan to fare a bit better than Europe here.

Other historical signposts of transportation-caused shifts can be seen in the United States. The growth and decay of major corporations and public policy shifts followed changes in transportation. After the policy shift in the Jacksonian era, investor-owned U.S. railroad companies became the dominant political and economic institutions of the nineteenth century as governments moved away from direct transportation development and began to either regulate or ignore railroads. This continued for half a century, until rail corporation abuses became impossible to ignore and public cries for reform were heard within the Progressive and Populist movements.[78] The railroads became stringently regulated just as technology caught up with them. Their monopoly of transportation eroded and their corporations declined as the life-style of the nation changed.

The result was a massive economic and political shift. Fortunes shifted on Wall Street and Main Street as the place of railroads as major private allocaters of public policy was largely taken over by automotive, petroleum, and air transport companies. Once the land-grant programs ended, the government began to heavily subsidize other modes of transportation without subsidizing railroads equally. The powerful new transport firms were influencing public policy in their own interests, just as their rail predecessors had done. Again, the political economy was rocked by shifts in transportation.

Transportation problems continue to play a critical role in the world. The difficulty of moving food and medicine for famine relief in sub-Saharan Africa is one example. The lack of transportation infrastructures allows vital relief supplies to build up at airports and docks while people in the hinterlands continue to starve. The decline of American automobile manufacturing in the face of foreign competition, the re-introduction of urban rail mass transit in North America's crowded cities, and the advocacy of state-developed high speed intercity rail passenger systems in the United States show that earthbound transportation is still a viable concern in the space age.

Transportation has a host of benefits for society.[79] Good freight transport allows consumers to benefit from geographic specialization, a territorial division of labor that increases efficiency. Other benefits frequently cited include the promotion of large-scale production (which requires bulk transportation of raw materials and finished goods) and the increase of the value of land adjacent to transportation services. Cumulatively, these transportation effects increase competition among sellers and foster the components of modern economic development.[80] They are crucial catalysts in industrial society.

Good transportation, especially of people, has desirable political effects as well. Economic development brought about by transportation speeds the settlement of frontier areas and fosters political cohesion in rapidly developing nations, encouraging nation-building and political integration.[81] Transportation is also a consolidating factor for already integrated polities, allowing patterns of social and political intercourse to become institutionalized. Transport is a key factor in national defense and modern war strategies, which depend on rapid troop and supply movements. That transportation infrastructures are prime targets in both strategic and guerilla warfare and the current Soviet (and projected U.S.) practice of basing mobile intercontinental missiles on trains illustrate transport's centrality in contemporary political struggles.

Harper makes these points quantitatively by citing how closely related are the volume of transportation demand and the condition of the economy in the United States. Transportation and related activities contributed approximately 11 percent of U.S. employment in 1976, the year of Conrail's birth.[82]

In summary, the American political economy has developed a set of transportation characteristics that separate it from most other industrialized systems. These have affected the development of American government involvement with railroads. In the United States, an infrastructure of common carrier private transportation firms dominates the political economy of transportation. Except as a response to economic and political emergencies, the public sector has eschewed providing transportation as a public utility as it has done in defense or environmental protection. Instead, routes, rates, safety, levels of service, modes of transportation employed, and so on have been determined by the marketplace, subject to inconsistent patterns of government regulation. As a result, transportation public policy has been heavily steered by those who seek to profit from it. It has developed an almost accidental character at times and has not benefited from significant long-range planning in pursuit of the public interest.

Rail transportation has some special roles and characteristics. A railroad "consists of two steel rails which are held a fixed distance apart upon a roadbed. Vehicles, guided and supported by flanged steel wheels, and connected into trains (or made into integral articulated units) are propelled as a means of transportation."[83] A railroad, then, is literally a road of rails upon which travel trains. In common parlance, however, the term "railroad" has come to embrace not only the actual tracks and trains, but transportation organizations such as Conrail and Amtrak, which use them to deliver goods and people over their rights of way. With the exception of a few private carriers, railroads in the United States (including government railroads like Amtrak) are organized as, at least potentially, for-profit corporations that rent or purchase and maintain their own rights of way, roadbeds, and rolling stock and solicit business as common carriers.

The origins of railroad technology are a matter of minor controversy. Some find a precursor in Roman roads with "standard gauge" stone ruts for chariots, medieval German mine tramways, and eighteenth-century Welsh mine tramways. By the end of the 1830s, railroading technology had progressed enough to harness iron rails and steam powered locomotives and make the railroad a practical commercial enterprise. As a result, rail companies sprang up all over the British Isles and the United States.

The technological characteristics of railroading cannot be divorced from the environment of the political economy.

Technological innovation has been the salvation of modern railroading in the United States, keeping it alive in spite of long years of managerial greed and abuse, punishing regulatory climates, and intense competition from subsidized competitors. Railroads remain efficient transportation providers in the automobile and air age because of the inherent physical efficiency of the flanged steel wheel running on steel rails.

Railroading has generated a culture and a mystique that surrounds and affects it to a degree not very well understood by contemporary financially oriented rail executives. This mystique has engendered generations of rail hobbyists, many of whom are well educated and in a position to influence public policy. The long presence of the railroad in the popular imagination and culture of the nation as well as its history has generated both negative and positive public awareness of railroading. As a result, rail issues generate more attention and controversy than the public's current fascination with the automobile and aerospace technology might logically predict.

Trains and railroaders have sustained the economies of many locales, from the "jerkwater" towns (places where steam locomotives made brief water stops) to medium sized cities like Altoona, Pennsylvania, and North Platte, Nebraska, which owe their existence to and are still very dependent upon the railroads that spawned them.[84] Railroads have made and broken industries of all sizes. Thus, it is not surprising that they have been the subject of intensely debated public policy and a common target for government intervention from their inception in England, the United States, and elsewhere.

The reason for this is simple. The railroad is an efficient, adaptable surface transportation system that has kept pace with technology. It is too important for policymakers to ignore. It has survived competition, adapted to many different forms of organization (public, quasi-public, and private), incorporated new technology (like the diesel-electric locomotive and continuous welded rail), and is usable on a desert, in a rain forest, on great plains, across a mountain range, and in a city, through virtually any kind of weather. It runs on many different kinds of fuel and is relatively cost effective across all of these tasks.

A railroad is not always profitable in its operations. Modern railroads are a transport mode with high social utility but a recurring problem of low economic return. Therefore, although railroads are a valued tool of all political economies, they are a problem for them as well.

On the plus side, railroads are efficient in land use, providing mass transportation of passengers and freight in urbanized environments with significantly less land impact and displacement than highways or even airport systems, in most cases. Railroads also discourage urban sprawl, dropping goods and people in central cities and spawning local feeder public transportation systems into them.[85]

Railroading is also energy efficient. In freight, it is thirty-seven times as efficient as air freight and far more efficient than trucks.[86] A typical piggyback train (with 1970s locomotives and a mixture of new light-weight and standard flat cars) carries trailers or containers using less than half as much fuel as the most efficient highway trucks. New microprocessor-controlled locomotives and light-weight cars do even better. In passenger service, trains are about four times more efficient than automobiles or commercial aircraft, but less efficient than intercity buses. Also, railroads can be propelled by energy from steam, coal, and nuclear, gas, or petroleum fuel, given some lead time for motive power conversion.

What is more, post-steam-era railroads are also highly labor efficient, using computerized dispatching and telemetry-equipped trains to beat all of their ground competitors, particularly on freight. In addition, they provide relatively safe and cost-effective transportation of hazardous or extremely heavy materials, keeping hazardous cargoes largely away from heavy passenger traffic and road-punishing bulk cargoes like coal or ore off public roads.

Modern railroads are far quieter than either their steam-era predecessors or their competition. New locomotives have quieting mechanisms that allow them to produce more power with less noise than highway trucks, when tire noise and rail wheel noise per given amount of tonnage is taken into account. Straight electric locomotives are far ahead in this respect, but they are less common in North America than they are in Europe and Japan. If grade crossings are eliminated (thus eliminating the need to sound air horns as often), rail noise performance would increase even more.

Linked with these fuel and noise efficiencies is the fact that railroads pollute the air less than highway trucks or jet cargo aircraft per ton mile and beat all but the most efficient and fully loaded intercity buses in passenger miles versus emissions. Railroads are far from perfect, of course. They still take up land, make noise, burn a lot of fuel, and pollute the air. They just do so relatively less than other forms of transportation with the exception of barges, which require deep waterways, locks, and dams.[87]

Hence, railroads in the current era of cross-country trains and microprocessor-equipped diesel-electric locomotives are less obtrusive transportation providers per like capacity than their competitors. That makes them socially desirable, although not always in favor with policymakers. Governments must concern themselves with importation of foreign energy, urban sprawl, air and water pollution, the social unrest caused by noise pollution, and a host of other problems endemic to industrial political economies. Inevitably, those nations like the United States that occasionally forget the social utility of railroads are forced to rediscover it when crises loom that can be best ameliorated by rail transportation. Future budgetary considerations coming from the huge federal deficits of the 1980s might even induce U.S. policymakers to reconsider the wisdom of subsidizing rail competitors while spending money to clean up after less efficient and dirtier alternatives.

As a result of this social utility, railroads quickly and extensively developed along with the industrial revolution and became a transportation monopoly in the last century. Technology reduced friction so effectively that even the first steam locomotives could pull far more than their own weight. Research and innovation made it economically feasible to lay tracks to places where customers resided. By providing a reliable guideway, the railroad rendered obsolete the need to put cargo in small, separate vehicles.[88] For these reasons, railroads developed sufficient social utility to capture large reservoirs of political support in spite of managerial abuses and public subsidies of competitors.

In spite of their continuing social utility and effective maintenance of a large political constituency (particularly outside of the United States), modern railroads are not operating on a clear track. They have a chronic problem in contemporary political economies of frequently being unable to attract enough revenues to pay for the cost of doing business. They meet their severest test in the marketplace and often fail it, dumping the problem in the lap of public policy. From a strict balance-sheet perspective, the efficiency of the flanged steel wheel on steel rail is spotty, given the enormous dollar costs of providing quality service and ignoring external social benefits. In a society like the United States, which eschews state ownership or subsidy of railroads (or in a society with scarce public resources, as in the developing world), this can be a major disadvantage.

Certain kinds of rail transportation are usually very profitable. Hauling of passengers in densely populated urban corridors where there is enough business to justify fast and frequent (usually electrified) service usually generates profits, according to economists.[89] The T.G.V. line in France, the Shinkansen service in Japan, and the Northeast Corridor Service in the United States are prominent examples, although exact operating results are closely guarded secrets of the governments involved due to political constraints. Similarly, hauling of freight for long distances with few intermediate stops and little need for marshalling and demarshalling of trains at terminals or along the way is economically viable. Single-commodity, permanently coupled unit trains and the generally long hauls that characterize the American and Canadian West fall into this category, as does transcontinental "land bridge" service for seagoing containers on flat cars which connects ships on both coasts.

For the rest of railroading, however, profits are harder to earn. The hauling of passengers outside of populous corridors generally loses money, in spite of the need for connections to sustain the profitability of high-speed express trains. Long-distance passengers expect food, sleeping accommodations, and other creature comforts that are labor intensive and therefore costly. Such trains also require increased roadbed maintenance expenses for smoothness and safety.

Short-haul freight trains also require large crews for switching, expensive classification yards, and a fleet of switch locomotives for individual loading dock pickup and delivery.

Light-density branch lines and small shipments are relatively expensive to service, though some short lines have proven that it can be done profitably if costs are pared rigorously.

This situation constitutes a problem for railroads and policy-makers. In spite of the socially desirable aspects of rail services, governments are often forced to subsidize them or run them directly, and railroads frequently petition regulatory authorities in enhanced free-market political economies to drop services with great social utility. Even quasi-nationalized railroads operate this way.[90] Private railroaders want either to make a profit or to get out of the railroad business. Consequently, governors are faced with the choice of subsidies, national-ization, or support of competing modes of transportation with less social utility.

Ultimately, railroads exist in an operating environment that is as much political as economic. They are causes and effects of political economy. The railroad has continued to maintain its position as a transportation provider that is valuable in society and has an effective constituency in the United States and elsewhere. While still the victim of ill-will and public distrust engendered by robber-baron era abuses and overshadowed by more glamorous forms of transportation, the railroad survives. In fact, it is currently experiencing one of its periodic renaissan-ces; this one is caused by the deregulation movement of the 1980s. It is fair to conclude that railroading's advantages have sustained it in spite of regulatory punishment, neglect, subsidy inequity vis-à-vis-competitors, and a host of self-inflicted wounds. It is an industry that refuses to die and that acts like a magnet in attracting government attention as governments attempt to discover and implement the public interest in contemporary political economies.

chapter three

Past Policies and Present Legacies

T HE PUBLIC POLICIES AFFECTING RAILROADS are not random occurrences. Regulation of private railroads and direct government forays into railroading are responses to the past and to definitions of present and future needs based upon perceptions of the past. Consequently, they are inseparable from the Hersonian politics of ideas[1] of the nation. Such important contemporary government rail policies as the creation and privatization of Conrail, the continuing quasi-nationalization of Amtrak, and the economic deregulation embodied in the Staggers Rail Act of 1980[2] emanate from public policy choices and from precedents of a century and a half of American political economy. This chapter focuses on those past policies and their present legacies and attempts to tie them together, using the theoretical approaches developed in chapters 1 and 2.

The History of U.S. Rail Public Policy

In his analysis of the failure of Conrail's immediate predecessor, the Penn Central Transportation Company, Sobel[3] argues that the "fateful choices" made in the century and a half before Conrail's start-up had as much to do with the form Conrail (and other rail policy legacies) took as did the financial and operating machinations of Penn Central management. Other analysts agree.[4]

Discussing the policies of the Andrew Jackson administration (including Jackson's influential secretary of state and successor, Martin Van Buren) toward government construction, ownership, and operation of basic transportation infrastructures, Sobel notes that it was typical Jacksonian transport policy to veto a congressional appropriation for a federal road in Kentucky. Jackson slowed and almost starved the National Road project and withdrew the federal government from the canal business with vetoes of appropriations for the Chesapeake and Ohio and Louisville and Portland canals, promising that similar proposals would meet the same fate. Since these decisions came just as railroads were becoming economically viable, they were significant precedents.

Jackson's policies were deliberate and unambiguous. "The federal government would not take the lead in becoming directly involved in the financing and operating of major transportation projects. New turnpikes and canals — and future railroads — would either receive state and local support or be privately financed, controlled, and operated, perhaps under the supervision of state legislatures.... Whatever would take place, the federal government rejected responsibility and leadership [on transportation development] in the Jackson years ... and all the while, Philadelphia and Baltimore, which needed federal assistance for their projects, would fall farther behind in the race [with New York] for continental domination."[5]

The Jacksonian precedents continue to have impact in the current era, leading to the privatization of Conrail and the efforts of the Reagan administration to dismantle Amtrak. Jackson's opposition to government enterprise nurtured an anti-government sentiment already present in the political culture of the U.S. political economy and turned it into an enduring public policy toward transportation. His opposition to the national bank (Bank of the United States, located in Philadelphia) and his alliance with Van Buren and his New York constituency (with a state-financed Erie Canal to ship goods into the interior and eclipse Philadelphia commercially) developed into a general public policy of limited involvement of the national government in transportation. Thus, the young nation set upon a course of transportation policy markedly different from that of Europe, Canada, and Japan.

In this policy environment, the major railroads of the United States were born and matured as private, profit-seeking firms. It was a major factor in their strengths, their abuses, and their subsequent regulatory treatment by state and national governments. It also contributed to their eventual failure to compete with federally subsidized competition by trucks, buses, barges, and airlines. These transportation modes developed later and matured in an era of transportation policy that still eschewed nationalization but embraced subsidy for new transportation modes.

The original pre-Jacksonian policy of the national government to treat transportation as a public utility and to develop a nationally owned and operated transport infrastructure (for economic development) gave way to privatization without significant regulation by the 1830s. In Sobel's words, "a combination of Jacksonian events — the rejection of the public transportation network, the creation of a speculatory boom following the [1833] disestablishment of the national bank and the rapid payment of the national debt — seemed to assure that the railroads, then an infant industry, would be constructed through private, not public, enterprise.... Even though the federal government would later help the railroads in many ways, there was no chance of a federal rail line along the model of the national road."[6]

The logical implications of such a public policy were obvious: "... there would be no integrated railroad network, but instead a patchwork of roads, each developing according to local needs at first, and then coming together due to changes in markets, technology, personnel, politics, and vision."[7]

All of this was clearly discernible by the 1840s, as railroads began to develop in earnest, fueled by technology and national growth.[8] The early and inconsistent efforts of states and some local governments to step into the vacuum left by the exit of the federal government from transportation development were soon all but abandoned due to lack of resources, shared laissez-faire cultural sentiments of state and local officials, and their inability to compete with private investors and speculators on both sides of the Atlantic. Today, only a few isolated fossils of that era remain, such as the ownership (but not operation) of a part of the Norfolk Southern system by the city of Cincinnati and the municipal ownership of the New Orleans Public Belt Railroad. This left allocation of the new and efficient rail technology to essentially unregulated capitalism, with all of its advantages and disadvantages.

Subsequent technological developments and public policies changed the environment of railroading significantly. But the present rail quasi-nationalizations and public promotions of other transportation modes have had less cumulative impact on the transportation system of the United States than these seminal precedents. The die was cast for a privately owned U.S. rail system during the critical decade of the 1830s.

The rail system that matured during the pre-regulatory period (before the development and strengthening of the Interstate Commerce Commission) was characterized by rapid growth and predatory practices. The era of political economy it engendered came to be known as the "robber-baron" era, as private rail moguls developed their empires in an atmosphere of great vision, technological talent, managerial expertise, courage, and fanatical dedication of purpose, as well as fraud, greed, ruthlessness, and manipulation.[9]

The development of the Pennsylvania and the New York Central, both Conrail ancestors, is typical. They gobbled up rivals and extended their rails westward, deciding where the rails would go and which areas would develop. They acted as important industrial and economic development catalysts for their Philadelphia and New York bases. Taking advantage of the functional absence of competition of competing transportation modes and the lack of national planning or effective regulation, they competed with each other, setting the scene for later problems.

The Pennsylvania, later to be known as "the standard railroad of the world" by friend and foe alike, was the clear leader in technology and service in the early years. Its fiscally conservative management also avoided most financial machinations as well. This policy was followed in order to keep its Philadelphia blue-blood stockholders happy and secure with their dividends and to relieve pressure on management.

The New York Central, however, had financial resources that far surpassed those of the Pennsylvania because of its New York base. It eventually grew faster and bigger (but not necessarily sounder) than the Pennsylvania. Despite their differences, both railroads paid little attention to stockholders and governments in their day-to-day operating plans. This left them free to compete with other railroads and each other, and led to the development of a "public be damned" attitude.[10]

This competition was not always relentless and irrational. It did produce enterprise and technological innovation. Also, the railroads made numerous attempts at intercompany cooperation out of self-interest. In the nineteenth century there were even some extended periods of detente between rival rail empires, including these two systems. Major stockholders' interests were occasionally considered in management policies during the formative and growth years of the systems. Nevertheless, the prevailing ethic was one of almost complete managerial independence and proprietary selfishness by managers. Their extensive autonomy was a luxury that their rail descendents and other industrial captains would not enjoy.

With the arrival of the unfettered free-enterprise era in the latter half of the nineteenth century, the New York Central and the Pennsylvania railroads became major parts of the emerging American laissez-faire political economy. Led by such giants as Cornelius Vanderbilt and J. P. Morgan of the New York Central and J. Edgar Thompson of the Pennsylvania, these major railroads reached the zenith of their economic freedoms and political influence. They intimidated or bought legislatures almost at whim and drove ever westward, ignoring all signs of public discontent, with few pressures to consider the public interest.

The excesses and machinations of this period of transportation history have been well documented elsewhere, so it is not necessary to detail them here. Two points will suffice: the excesses of the Pennsylvania and the New York Central were not as extensive or as serious as those of the owners of the Erie and other systems, but the excesses were real. The lack of concern for the public and stockholders and the abuses of public interest on the part of the entire rail industry contributed to a major shift in public policy from one of laissez-faire to first halting and then increasingly heavy (and even punitive, at times) government regulation. The public organized and demanded protection from the robber barons, and politicians eventually responded. Unfortunately, the heirs of those politicians have not always adjusted those responses to new realities. Eventually, this weakened railroads generally, in spite of their national utility.

The initial responses in the 1880s of policymakers to the problem of the robber barons were tepid and halting. Specific abuses were addressed in ways that were deliberately limited and designed not to provoke too much wrath from these very powerful special interests. By the turn of the century, however, the power of antirailroad special interests like the Grangers had grown enough to command a legislative presence and to take on the prevailing laissez-faire cultural imperatives of the political economy.[11] This moved the regulators to gradually erect a barrier against rail management abuses that effectively became a straitjacket for these once-imperious firms.

As subsidized competitors for railroads emerged and as railroads were prevented from responding to them effectively, the fortunes of the railroads declined precipitously. Even the national prosperity of the 1920s did not help them significantly, and the Great Depression put half their locomotives in storage. Few routes escaped the ravages of deferred maintenance and bankruptcy in this period.

Only national public policy could rescue the situation for the public interest. It is an irony that the excesses of private railroad owners were nurtured by a laissez-faire policy that set in motion a chain of events that eventually led to the direct government involvement in the rail political economy that the original policy eschewed so vigorously. Before the apogee of the robber-baron era, railroads had been regulated by state and local governments. As relatively weak new concerns that had to traverse many jurisdictions, railroads were bedeviled by attempts of governments of all sizes to control their land-grabbing. Governments were willing to reap the advantages the railroads could bring, but they felt justified in regulating them. Since the national government had opted out of the process and since the railroads were yet weak, the result was a patchwork of local laws and regulations, often petty and inevitably conflicting from jurisdiction to jurisdiction.

The railroad moguls eventually overcame their policy disadvantage by a combination of economic power, graft, and occasional appeals to reason. By the 1870s, their power had far outstripped that of various sub-national governments, which lacked jurisdiction sufficient to cope with the railroads' new ability to allocate public policy.

Had they been wise enough to exercise restraint, the rail moguls might have kept their power indefinitely and been able to take advantage of the political culture by blocking much emerging regulation and by holding technology at bay, at least temporarily. Restraint was not one of the virtues of the robber barons, however. Their excesses gave their victims the weapons to kill the goose that had laid such a laissez-faire golden egg.

What the earlier railroad victims of the East had not been able to accomplish by themselves (in spite of some heroic efforts) was finally done by the farmers of the West. They organized themselves into grass-roots political clubs called granges. These organizations became adept at lobbying and power-brokering and used their newfound power principally to protect themselves against their railroad predators. They were dependent upon the railroads for economic well-being, but suffered from railroad manipulations that denied the very well-being the existence of rails made possible. Thus, farmers exercised their clout to force midwestern legislators to enact strong laws against railroad rate discrimination favoring powerful shippers, free passes to the privileged, watered stock, and other abuses.

Soon, these successful state efforts were felt in Washington. The transportation policy of the nation began to move away from the precedents of the Jacksonian era as policymakers perceived changing times and developed a different concept of the public interest. Congress finally began to respond to pressures just as state legislatures had done. The first breakthrough came in 1887 when Senator Shelby M. Cullom of Illinois pushed through legislation creating what came to be the bane of the railroads' collective existence, the Interstate Commerce Commission.[12] The original commission was empowered to regulate against discriminatory rates, pooling of loads for favored customers, rebates, and other abuses of railroad customers. It also required railroads to make their rates public and to post them, another effort to prevent collusion.[13]

As significant as these departures were, the new commission still had limited powers. It could not fix rates, for example, and was handed defeat after defeat on the extent of its authority by the Supreme Court. In effect, the early I.C.C. was quarantined by the railroads, albeit temporarily. The public policy tide had clearly turned against laissez-faire railroading by the end of the nineteenth century. The Grangers and their allies, the Progressives, began to dominate American politics in the new century and to retaliate against their former victimizers.

Even though eastern railroads like the Pennsylvania and the New York Central did not serve Granger territory for the most part, they were not immune from the public policy efforts of the Grangers' lobbying. Feeling the effects of regulation, they retaliated by raising rates precipitously, slashing wages, and treating their customers and stockholders with more disdain than ever. Railway labor resisted the wage cuts, adding to the list of troubles the rail moguls faced as a legacy of their immoderation. The violent railway strikes of the late 1870s and beyond led to scores of deaths in Pittsburgh and elsewhere at the hands of railroad-hired guards and of federal troops. They also led directly to the rapid growth of the railway brotherhoods, the powerful railroad workers' unions which were to eventually plague the railroads in later hard times.

Collectively, these events resulted in the weakening of the once-mighty railroads to the detriment of the national interest. It had become good electoral politics to be antirailroad. Adding to the troubles brought about by antirailroad court cases, American railroads became targets of a national antirailroad legislative momentum.[14] The weakening of the Interstate Commerce Commission by the still-impressive rail legislative clout in 1887 (with subsequent assistance from the U.S. Supreme Court) was reversed by a series of acts emanating from Congress in the years before World War I. Starting with the Elkins Act of 1903 and accelerated by the Hepburn Act of 1906 and the Mann-Elkins Act of 1910, the Interstate Commerce Commission was shored up and given sweeping enforcement powers to use against the railroads.[15]

In retrospect, what had been a sensible attempt to curb railroad abuses with legislation combined with a policy of vigorous antitrust legislation and enforcement gradually turned into a successful crusade by affected interests to induce public-policy-makers to punish and debilitate the railroads. By the beginning of the First World War and the subsequent experience of temporary nationalization of railroads, the power of the robber-barons had been permanently curbed. The prewar period was one of steep decline for railroads.[16] This was accomplished so thoroughly that the public policy reversal to probusiness in the 1920s under Harding, Coolidge, and Hoover had little or no effect on the railroads' fortunes. Railroads had been so thoroughly damaged that they could not cope effectively with an easing of regulation and take advantage of prosperity.

Simultaneously with punitive regulation, the railroads faced real competition for the first time. The technology of flanged steel wheel running on steel rail had given the railroads an enormous advantage in the middle of the nineteenth century. Neither wagon nor canal had serious hopes of competing with the steam-locomotive-drawn train that was virtually immune to grade, weather, or distance by the turn of the century. However, technology did not stand still for railroad competitors. The development of the internal combustion engine soon gave birth to buses, trucks, and passenger automobiles. Though primitive at first, just as early railroad motive power had been, they developed rapidly. What is more, they did not face laissez-faire transportation policies. The federal government, starting with the 1916 Federal Air Road Act and the 1921 Federal Highway Act, began a policy of backing emerging transportation modes with subsidized rights of way.[17] The government wanted to foster rapid economic development and to give the railroads some competition. Later, the airline and barge industries would get the same treatment. Taken together, this aid would far surpass anything the railroads received in land grants during the post-Civil War era. This aid continues to the present; the railroads are still forced to own and develop their own taxed rights-of-way, while their competitors get free rights-of-way (with no taxes associated with them) in return for user fees and taxes that cover only a small percentage of their true worth.

The railroads' technological advantage had seemingly disappeared. Certainly, the railroads' monopoly had disappeared in the transportation political economy of the twentieth century. The efficiency of rail technology remained, however, and would remanifest itself later, in spite of policy-assisted competition from other transport modes. When regulatory relief changed the situation in the 1980s, the rail advantage resurfaced as Conrail and other railroads took the offensive against long-haul trucks and were successful in winning back much business they had earlier lost.[18] The regulatory imbalances have effectively masked the railroads' advantages in fuel efficiency, labor costs, and all-weather reliability, but these advantages never disappeared as other technologies developed.

By the beginning of World War I, the burden of regulation exacted a massive toll on the railroads. They entered the war with a deteriorated physical plant and demoralized management. While the U.S. Railway Administration's legacy included the positive elements of efficient steam locomotive designs and some quality physical plant rehabilitation, the demands of the war took their toll on the railroads, and the federal government did not return rail properties to the private owners' managements in substantially better shape than it had found them.[19]

The swift postwar return of American railroads to private ownership promptly re-ignited the debate on the rail nationalization on the European model, which had accompanied previous regulatory episodes of public policy. The Plumb Plan for nationalization, drafted by a railroad labor lawyer, was introduced in Congress and was seriously debated. It was supported by such groups as the Public Ownership League of America and by organized rail labor. It was opposed by the railroads' "former" owners and by shippers, who wanted to divide and conquer the rail companies. It failed to pass Congress not so much because of debating points made in the Capitol but because of the powerful influence of the culture of the American political economy. Nationalization was still anathema, despite the successful experience during the war.

American railroads reverted to their previous privately owned form with the passage of the Transportation Act of 1920.[20] The law also redefined the powers of the Interstate Commerce Commission so that railroads were given some revenue relief in order to help them emerge from the financial doldrums that resulted from the policies of earlier years.

The act also mandated a plan designed to foster mergers to ensure the survival of fewer, more viable railroads. Like the

Plumb Plan, the rationalization plan was not translated into effective public policy; the Interstate Commerce Commission failed to pursue it as squabbling and jealousies among rail managers surfaced.[21] By 1921, the plan had essentially withered away, its legislative mandate ignored with the tacit consent of all concerned. The overall effect of the act was to foster a marginal rail recovery, but railroads fared far less well than other industries in the booming decade of the 1920s.

With the advent of the Great Depression, U.S. railroads virtually collapsed. They had no reserves upon which to draw as revenues declined following the decline of national industrial output. Locomotives were put in storage (about half the total fleet at the height of the Depression), and bankruptcies became common. Of the seven hundred railroad companies in business in 1933, one hundred either disappeared outright or were gobbled up in forced mergers during the next six years. Over one thousand miles of track were abandoned each year from 1932 to 1943, shrinking the size of the total system to what it was in 1912.[22] Passenger service was allowed to deteriorate most, since it was more expensive to maintain than the freight business. The ravages of deferred maintenance, aging equipment, depressed revenues, and increased competition from other modes of transportation were indeed devastating. Pullman and parlor-car fare surcharges, initiated by the federal government during World War I were never repealed, precipitating a decline of that service, for example.[23] Many passenger trains were taken out of service permanently in this period, and the premier rail passenger network in the world lost its edge.

Because of the general collapse, the plight of the rails caught the attention of public-policy-makers once again. Despite the sympathy of the Roosevelt administration to government intervention in principle, the strength of the laissez-faire culture of the American political economy prevailed. Proposed remedies including nationalization and/or drastic rationalization and subsidy surfaced, were duly debated, and laid to rest. Again, the result was the failure to implement a long-term public policy for railroad rationalization.

As the Depression gave way before the onslaught of World War II production, the fortunes of the rails improved along with other sectors of the economy. U.S. Railway Administration style nationalization was not seriously considered as a response to the looming emergency, and the still-private railroads responded to the war effort patriotically and efficiently, given their condition. They moved prodigious, record-setting amounts of traffic and even did some physical-plant rehabilitation. However, the demands of wartime traffic outstripped the advantages of wartime revenues, and the rail infrastructure of the nation re-entered peacetime in exhausted condition. There were no national public policies for revival and renewal, and the rail owners had none either. The status quo had returned to a rail political economy that was essentially unchanged by the war and the Depression.

Decline continued in the 1950s and 1960s. In spite of the flash of proxy fights and a few serious attempts, like the introduction of the lightweight Aerotrain and western streamliners, to lure passenger traffic back to the rails, automobiles, airplanes, and trucks proliferated and the railroads deteriorated. Railroads remained largely antipassenger in this period[24] and seemed incapable of halting their steadily declining share of intercity freight as well. The public policy of subsidizing competitors while regulating railroads in waves of inconsistent strength and duration, which had emerged ad hoc in the twentieth century, resulted in more deferred maintenance and service cutbacks. Even the rapid introduction of the diesel-electric locomotive in the late forties and early fifties (resulting in the scrapping of nearly new steam locomotives) only temporarily staved off the inevitable. Railroads actively pursued passenger train abandonment, further contracted freight lines, and argued interminably with the Interstate Commerce Commission over every rate-hike or line-abandonment proposal.

During the postwar years, interstate highway development and air route system modernization accelerated, and the railroads declined further, particularly in the Northeast. Their customers went out of business or fled south. The result was a series of bankruptcies and defensive mergers through which the rails hoped to rationalize their redundancies and compete effectively with each other and other transportation modes. The Transportation Act of 1920 had been an unsuccessful attempt at merger via public policy. Now the desperate railroads pursued voluntary mergers.[25] While such a course of action might have been successful in the 1920s because the freight and passenger business was there and the railroads had the financial resources to take advantage of efficiencies gained, it was insufficient in the 1960s and 1970s. The mergers resulted in fewer Class I (large) railroads and the emergence of several huge systems. These were side-by-side mergers that often put two or more weak companies together to form one big weak company. The beneficial economies of scale from consolidation were offset by line redundancies, which regulatory authorities would not allow to be ameliorated, and by intramural rivalry. (An appreciation of the scope and effects of this merger movement on Conrail can be seen in the chronology following in this chapter.)

Along with these defensive mergers and some capital investment, the response of railroads was to press for sweeping regulatory reform, a cessation of subsidies to competitors, and relief from passenger service, which had become uneconomic in most places due to competition and decades of neglect. During the 1950s, and 1960s, the government policy response was either to ignore the problems of the railroads or to dole out regulatory relief in a piecemeal and insufficient fashion. The virtual collapse of large sectors of the American rail system finally forced real changes in public policy by the 1970s.

While a system-wide renaissance would not happen for the industry until the passage of the Staggers Rail Act of 1980, the initiation of quasi-nationalized passenger service and the bankruptcy of northeastern railroads began a new era in the public policy of railroading in the United States. The passage in 1976 of the Railroad Revitalization and Regulatory Reform Act brought a small amount of regulatory relief for all U.S. railroads. It was merely a prelude to the 1980 Staggers Act, however. That landmark legislation repealed the previous regulatory era and allowed railroads to compete with trucks on a more equal footing. A rational public policy toward transportation was emerging, and its effects were swift and sure: the decline of American railroads was halted and a turnaround began.

Before we turn to an extended case-brief of Conrail, case-briefs of Amtrak and Staggers, and lesser analyses of other current legacies of rail public policy in the United States, a conceptual summary and perspective is in order. Several generalizations emerge that are helpful in examining the present legacies of past public policies.

American rail public policy was largely nondirect and inconsistent until recently. Before the 1970s, the government regulated private transportation providers in waves of heavy and light regulation. It eschewed the direct involvement common elsewhere. Except for brief state and local direct excursions into railroading in the pre-Jacksonian era, the temporary nationalization during World War I, and other minor episodes like the Alaska Railroad nationalization, the public policy of the United States has been to regulate rather than operate railroads.

The 1970s, however, marked a turning point in this public policy. That was a decade of great uncertainty and sweeping changes in the American rail political economy. Given the failure of private, for-profit rail common carriers to provide adequate intercity rail passenger service and the bankruptcies of important northeastern and midwestern rail freight systems, the nondirect public policy of allowing regulated private railroads to allocate national rail transportation services for the public was abandoned de facto, even though no pronouncement to that effect was issued. In rapid succession, Uncle Sam formed a federal passenger railroad and a huge freight railroad. Within a six year period, U.S. rail policy integrated regulation by quasi-nationalization with nondirect regulation. At the same time, the wisdom of economically regulating private rail corporations began to be doubted, and the notion was abandoned with the passage of the Staggers Act four years after the establishment of Conrail. Thus, the government made dual regulatory choices. It decided to intervene directly when the market could not cope with allocatory needs. It also decided to enhance the market by partial deregulation in those areas of the rail political economy where the market was judged to be potentially effective.

To make regulatory policy changes is not a simple process. Any type of regulation involves subsidiary policy choices once the decision to pursue it has been made. One of the most important steps is to define the nature and character of regulation itself. Regulation "takes many forms.... It generally involves a conscious attempt by an individual or a group to influence the behavior of other individuals or organizations."[26]

In this case, of course, the regulating group is the government and the target is railroads. "It is not always possible to separate different types of government regulation; all ... influence the opportunities, consequences, penalties, and rewards associated with alternative courses of action considered by decision makers.... [Each] takes many forms; each form has many dimensions."[27]

One of the regulatory choices forced upon public policy makers is whether to regulate by direct intervention (e.g., by quasi-nationalization) or by indirect means. The latter presents many subsidiary choices, the most important being what forms and depth of indirect regulation to embrace.

One of the most compelling of the many types of regulation available to governments is occupational safety regulation, laws and rules enacted to "reduce the antisocial fallout of the industrial system."[28] This common type of regulation (used extensively in the United States and untouched by the recent deregulatory movement) is designed to protect workers and the general public from irreversible environmental and occupational health damages by firms. It is, therefore, different from economic regulation designed to protect consumer interests from the largely reversible effects of prices, service levels, industry organization, and so on.

Stemming from this was a decision either to regulate the services of firms while letting the market allocate them or to go beyond that by assuming a market allocates effectively for the public interest only if it is enhanced by pro-competitive measures. Thus, antitrust regulation (designed to control entry into economic areas, to regulate mergers and firms sizes, and to create competition within an industry) is a common form of economic regulation in the United States. In a sense, it is macroregulatory, because it uses public policy more broadly than microregulatory strategies, which merely regulate services of all firms in an industry.

Once policymakers decide on the direction of regulation, decisions must be made about its scope. Alternatives can be conveniently arrayed upon a continuum. At one pole is a modestly enhanced free market, whereby the government regulates lightly (usually to control the ranges of specific abuses after they have become evident and are judged to be serious), thereby hoping to assist the natural regulatory forces of the market. This closely resembles the public policy of transportation deregulation now in place in the United States.[29]

Adjacent to enhanced free market on the continuum is heavier regulation, which effectively preempts the managerial prerogatives of private firms by mandating many economic duties and proscriptions. That resembles the pre-Staggers era in the United States rail political economy. The government also can regulate by spin-off from other policies, like taxation, which provide economic incentives and disincentives for desirable behavior. More pervasively, government can regulate by example and competition through quasi-nationalization, next on the continuum, or nationalization, the pole opposite enhanced free market. By quasi-nationalizing or nationalizing a key firm in a given economic sector, the government may force competitive, privately owned firms to match public-firm price and performance standards. This resembles the role that the Tennessee Valley Authority plays in regional electrical power generating infrastructure or the role that Conrail played among private railroads when it was quasi-nationalized.

It is important to note that the American regulatory process itself has certain relevant characteristics. As we have already seen, policies and structures resist change[30] because interest groups find it relatively easy to block change within the American polity. Also, as Noll and Owen put it, "policy is made in the context of organized persuasive activity by competing interest groups with something to gain or lose from the outcome.... [They] provide regulators with information, analysis, and argument ... difficult or impossible for policymakers or their staffs to compile independently."[31] Thus, they develop patterns of relationships with regulators that can blur the sharp distinctions between client and regulator. Regulation can be used strategically by firms to handicap their competitors.[32] This allows those with power and cleverness another opportunity to bend regulatory policies to their own advantage. Well-represented interests have significant advantages in the adversarial proceedings of regulation in the United States. They are frequently successful in equating their narrow interests with the public interest due to the lack of effective representation for the other side(s).[33] Taken together, these characteristics give the regulatory process in the United States a momentum toward "stickiness" of regulations, toward big and well-organized economic interests, and away from the public interest.

Thus, the regulatory process itself is not neutral and should be evaluated as evidence for and against the advisability of given regulatory policies. Like any policy decision, the decision to form a quasi-nationalized railroad or to regulate indirectly must be put into effect through the policy process. Therefore, the characteristics and likely outcomes of the process are relevant.

Legacies of U.S. Rail Policy

Let us turn to the principal contemporary legacies of American public policy toward railroads — Conrail, Amtrak, the present regulatory climate (the Staggers era), and other, less-sweeping policies.

The Consolidated Rail Corporation

The birth of the Consolidated Rail Corporation at 12:01 A.M. on April 1, 1976, was not a chance occurrence. It was a predictable, if not inevitable, outcome of a century and a half of economic development, decay, and ad hoc public policy on transportation. As a major rail transportation provider, Conrail and its development and nurturing in the first decade of its existence is inseparable from the remainder of American railroading.

The Jacksonian-era decisions of government to abdicate responsibility for transportation development as a public utility, the growth of Conrail's ancestor firms during the ensuing period of free reign of private enterprise, the inevitable backlash against these firms in the era of heavy regulation, the development and governmental nurturing of competition for railroads, the deterioration of rail properties and their financial worth, and the emergence of at least a temporary movement toward federal rationalization of transportation policies during the present era all affected Conrail. Even though Conrail postdated these developments, they affected it as much as or more than they did private railroads such as the Union Pacific or CSX.

The Pennsylvania and the New York Central railroads were the principal operational, financial, and political components of the Conrail system. Their combination to form the Penn-Central Transportation Company in 1968 and its shocking (but predictable) failure just two years later were the immediate catalysts for the intense political activity leading to the passage of a law creating Conrail in 1974, the acceptance by Congress of the U.S.R.A. Final System Plan in 1975, and the actual startup in 1976.

The Pennsylvania declined less precipitously during the 1930s than did the New York Central because of better management and a slightly more lucrative freight customer network. The Central's losses during the Depression amounted to a virtual hemorrhage of its capital. The Pennsy, on the other hand, showed a slight profit (at least on paper) for the duration of the 1930s and even managed to electrify what would eventually become Amtrak's Northeast Corridor. The railroad continued to pay dividends, keeping up its long-standing tradition of buying managerial autonomy with the coin of dividends. In reality, however, the Philadelphia management team did no better than hold the status quo during that perilous decade. Both railroads had succumbed to the weakness intrinsic to American railroads and were vulnerable to eventual collapse.

Except for a hiatus during World War II, these and other Conrail predecessor companies continued to decline along with most of American railroading. Though their managements tried to arrest the decline by merging the two eastern giants, it was a case of too little, too late. Even public policy hurt the new merger — it was delayed for a fatal period by the Interstate Commerce Commission and then, upon its acceptance, was further poisoned by the forced inclusion of the extremely weak New York, New Haven, and Hartford Railroad with its money-losing commuter services. If 1980s-style deregulation had been enacted at least fifteen years earlier, perhaps the Penn-Central merger would have restored financial health to these railroads and Conrail's turnaround would have been Penn-Central's, in spite of managerial bungling. It was not to be, however, and the Penn-Central was doomed before its birth by events that preceded it, and bungling only hastened the inevitable. The other bankrupt northeastern and midwestern railroads that entered Conrail in 1976 were similarly doomed.

The 1976 Annual Report of Conrail contained an interesting chronology, shown in figure 3.1,[34] which shows what the public, the federal government, Conrail employees, competing transportation systems, and shippers faced when the Penn-Central collapsed. This chronology, written early in 1977, did not include the 1980 passage of the Staggers Act to strengthen and extend the Railroad Revitalization and Regulatory Reform Act.

The chronology gives the development of and impact of the bankruptcies and the timetable (swift in retrospect) of public-sector response to them. The bankruptcies precipitated a crisis of major proportions, threatening the existence of over half the rail capacity of the heavily populated and industrialized northeastern quadrant of the United States. They also threatened the supply lines of the automobile, mining, and steel industries.

Economic crisis loomed because of the plight of the rail system and, once again, cries were raised for nationalization and/or radical rationalization, activating the policy processes. This time, however, the problems were so acute and the public sector had so few alternatives that the cries for major rationalization were heeded in spite of their seeming cultural incongruence. Another quasi-nationalization followed Amtrak, and the beginning of the end of an old regulatory era resulted. Conrail's birth and the Staggers Act emanated from the ill-begotten union of the Pennsylvania and the Central, and ultimately from the actions of Jackson, Van Buren, Thompson, and Morgan.

The events that led to the formation of the Consolidated Rail Corporation were similar to those that led to the formation of the National Railroad Passenger Corporation. In both cases, there were no other viable options for those entrusted with administering the public interest. Decades of poor policy choices and inertia had made the scenario inevitable well before the 1970s. Congressional reaction was necessary and unavoidable (though it should be noted that Congress could have made worse choices and postponed the inevitable).

Freight railroading, particularly in the economically declining Northeast and Midwest, had fallen on hard times by the time of the Penn Central merger. The heavy industrial base that generated rail traffic had eroded. The trucking industry was

THE EVOLUTION OF CONRAIL

Start-up dates of predecessor railroads and steps toward conveyance day.

Origins

October 7, 1826

Conrail's oldest segment, Granite Railway Co., built to carry granite blocks for the Bunker Hill Monument from a quarry in West Quincy, Mass. Through successive mergers became part of New York, New Haven & Hartford Railroad, a predecessor of Penn Central.

First car on first railroad

June 6, 1829

Schuylkill Valley Navigation and Railroad Co., oldest segment of Reading Company.

Early Reading steam engine

August 9, 1831

Mohawk and Hudson Railroad, oldest portion of New York Central Railroad, a Penn Central predecessor.

October, 1832

Camden & Amboy Railroad & Transportation Co., earliest segment of Pennsylvania Railroad, a predecessor of Penn Central.

January 1, 1842

Elizabethtown & Somerville Railroad Co., oldest line of Central Railroad Co. of New Jersey.

May 14, 1851

New York & Erie Railroad, oldest segment of Erie Railroad, a predecessor of Erie Lackawanna Railroad.

M&HRR

"John Bull" historic locomotive preserved in Smithsonian

October 15, 1851

Lackawanna & Western Railroad, original line of Delaware, Lackawanna & Western Railway Co., an Erie Lackawanna predecessor.

Phoebe Snow, legendary Lackawanna trade mark

June 11, 1855

Delaware, Lehigh, Schuylkill & Susquehanna Railroad, earliest line of Lehigh Valley Railroad Co.

1880s-1920s

Prosperity

Railroads, as America's primary mode of freight transportation, prospered, as a whole.

August 14, 1882

Lehigh & Hudson River Railway Co. stock held by other five predecessor railroads in Conrail.

February 1, 1968

Penn Central Transportation Co. created by merger of Pennsylvania Railroad and New York Central Railroad.

1930s-1960

Decline

Competitive modes, supported in part (directly and indirectly) by enormous government financial resources, severely cut into railroads' profitability and traffic; railroads' capital resources declined (especially in the Northeast Quadrant of America); maintenance expenditures were deferred.

October 17, 1960

Erie Lackawanna Railway Co. formed by merger of Erie Railroad and Delaware, Lackawanna & Western Railroad.

March 22, 1967

Bankruptcies

Central Railroad of New Jersey entered bankruptcy.

November 23, 1971

Reading Company entered bankruptcy.

July 24, 1970

Lehigh Valley Railroad Co. declared bankruptcy.

June 21, 1970

Penn Central entered bankruptcy.

December 31, 1968

New York, New Haven & Hartford Railroad included in Penn Central.

January 2, 1974

President Nixon signed Regional Rail Reorganization Act into law, calling it a "turning point in history," following Congressional passage on December 21, 1973.

February 8, 1973

One-day labor strike shuts down Penn Central; government intervention ends strike, setting in motion process of government participation to resolve dilemma of rail bankruptcies in Northeast.

Government Action

June 26, 1972

Erie Lackawanna Railway Co. entered bankruptcy.

April 18, 1972

Lehigh & Hudson River Railway Co. filed for bankruptcy.

74

May 2, 1974

Penn Central, Reading, Central Railroad of New Jersey and Lehigh Valley ruled unreorganizable by their respective bankruptcy courts.

December 16, 1974

Supreme Court found RRRA Constitutional by 7-2 vote.

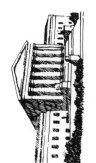

February 26, 1975

United States Railway Association's Preliminary System Plan for restructuring bankrupt lines released. Called for 15,000 route-mile system, including 3,400 miles of light density lines, and expanded Norfolk & Western and Chessie System to provide competition.

April 16, 1975

Special Appeals Court in Washington upheld Erie Lackawanna Reorganization Court decision to allow late inclusion of EL in Conrail.

November 9, 1975

USRA's Final System Plan for Conrail (filed with Congress on July 28, 1975) is accepted by Congress.

Final System Plan

January 28, 1976

Railroad Revitalization and Regulatory Reform Act passed Congress (signed by President Ford on February 5) amending the RRRA.

Quad R Act

March 12, 1976

Financing Agreement between USRA and Conrail concluded. Conrail has access to government investment funds up to $2.026 billion to launch operations.

$2 Billion

April 1, 1976

Rail properties conveyed to Conrail at 12:01 a.m.

Conrail Begins

CONRAIL

taking full advantage of the Interstate Highway network and a permissive regulatory climate to win business away from the railroads. The regulatory climate facing railroads, on the other hand, made it difficult or impossible for them to shed excess trackage capacity, annul money-losing passenger trains, or to enter into competitive rate contracts with major shippers to regain significant amounts of business. To make matters worse, railroads were not earning enough return on investment to generate sufficient capital to reinvigorate their deteriorating physical plant. Even maintaining the status quo, the genuine achievement of the Pennsylvania Railroad during the Depression, was no longer possible. Major rail systems, like the Pennsylvania and the New York Central, not only faced imminent bankruptcy, but also had an alarmingly poor capacity to provide safe transportation for the business left to them. This was detrimental to the public interest as well as the railroads.

Fred W. Frailey, assistant managing editor of *U.S. News and World Report*, put it this way:

> The next two decades after 1957 were not kind to the railroad [Pennsylvania]. These were years of shippers moving South and West, of oil and atomic power muscling in on coal as an energy source, of limited-access highways, of cars, and German machine tools. Pennsy faltered through the 1950s. It stumbled through the 1960s. The 1968 merger ... ended in debacle two years later — a bankruptcy the size of which America had not seen before and hasn't seen since.
>
> Six painful years, each more demoralizing and hand to mouth than the last, passed before Congress reorganized the Penn Central and five other bankrupt Northeast railroads into Consolidated Rail Corporation, invested — ultimately — $3.3 billion in rehabilitation, and hoped for the best.[35]

The Conrail service area needed the cost advantages of rail freight service for its declining industrial base. With congressional delegations from the sixteen states originally represented in Conrail territory, there was a large political constituency demanding effective action, adding momentum to the drive to challenge the prevailing culture of the American political economy with the formation of a quasi-nationalized Conrail.

The other bankrupt railroads were not only in the same dire straits as the Penn Central, but also dependent on the rapidly deteriorating Penn Central for much of their traffic interchange. They suffered from the failure of policymakers to allow them to shed their share of the great overcapacity of rail lines in the region.

The congressional response was bold in the context of the culture and the events. Given the enormity of the problem, and the confusion, court challenges and delays that were caused by those with an interest in the problem trying to protect themselves, the public policy formulation and implementation response was swift. (This is especially true considering the incompetence, mismanagement, and outright financial shenanigans that characterized the collapse of the Penn Central.[36])

The political pressures accompanying these events were enormous. Though the events did not dominate headlines or influence elections, they caught and held the attention of policymakers and the affected interests. Rail nationalization had once again risen to a prominent place on the policy agenda because of the depths of the crisis and the unlikelihood of a private-enterprise solution. Major shippers and state and local officials made it clear that they would not accept wholesale abandonment and liquidation of the bankrupt railroads' properties (coupled with sale of the few desirable segments of the bankrupts to other railroads) under any conditions because of the unacceptably large gaps that would be left in the rail service. Congress got the message quickly, and subsequent legislation reflected the realization that there was no politically or economically acceptable set of conditions that could justify cessation of train service to most of the Midwest and Northeast.

Given the powerful sway of the political culture and the prevailing philosophies of the Republican administrations in the White House during this period, it is no surprise that explicit European-style nationalization was equally anathema. No national politician wanted to preside over the defeat of capitalism that nationalizing railroads would symbolize. Yet, the crisis was real, not symbolic. Reality demanded that something be done, and no true private-sector solution was available, in spite of the diligent search for one by many of the best minds along the Potomac and up the Northeast Corridor in Wall Street.

Thus, Congress, with the sometimes reluctant support of the Nixon administration, created Conrail as a quasi-nationalized, profit-seeking corporation virtually by default.[37] Nevertheless, it was a successful policy. It solved the problem with a combination of symbolism and reality. Conrail eventually was cost-effective, socially efficient, and kept the form of a private, for-profit corporation. However, Conrail's 85 percent ownership by the federal government and its open-ended access to the federal treasury for operating and rehabilitation funds in lieu of sufficient operating revenues meant that Conrail was not an ordinary private railroad. Its managerial independence and freedom from mandated social burdens gave it a unique semi-private, semi-nationalized structure that was its real strength. Free enterprise was grafted to the corpus of a nationalized corporation's resources. The result was the fortuitous, if perhaps accidental, melding of the best characteristics of each: the quasi-nationalization of seven U.S. railroads, which preserved service and turned a profit within five years.

In retrospect, Conrail's strengths and potentials were not widely appreciated. Its detractors far outnumbered its proponents. Though its corporate form was modeled vaguely upon that of Comsat and Amtrak,[38] the public policy that created Conrail still had to transcend culture and skepticism. The fact that it succeeded beyond the expectations of even its most optimistic architects caught most people by surprise. Conrail was a result of the combination of thorough grounding in rail history and political economy on the part of some congressional members and staffers and instinctual steps down the path of least resistance by others. It was business as usual in the sense that the federal government waited until a crisis loomed and then reacted quickly. What was different about this response, however, was a combination of congressional good judgment, wise-planning in a hurry for both the middle as well as the short range, and a set of options that were obviously the best public policy. Conrail's birth signalled a new era for U.S. rail policy.

While Conrail's official emergence as a corporate entity was in 1976, the disposal of nonrailroad property conveyed by the bankrupt companies to the government and settlements with their estates took many more years and involved expensive court fights. The new rail system inherited a mess. On its first day of operation, Conrail's physical plant (roadbed, signal and communication systems, classification yards, and so on) was in deplorable shape. Its rolling stock (locomotives, freight, and passenger cars) was in much worse shape than even the stock Amtrak had inherited four years earlier. It also faced shrinking markets, vast overcapacity of track (which was expensive to maintain, much less to rehabilitate), and a bloated labor force operating under unproductive work rules that, in many cases, went back to the days of steam locomotives. It also was saddled with the remnants of unprofitable commuter services.

All in all, the new Conrail was a poor excuse for a railroad. It should surprise no one that the new railroad was initially less than a success. Squabbling broke out between operating and management personnel of the former companies, which had poor leadership from some high-level executives who were not railroaders. Interminable delays occurred in transportation due to bad track and equipment that broke down on the road, and even while standing, as track structure collapsed under the weight of motionless trains. Conrail's image in the popular and rail press, as well as in the public eye, was poor, even though the seeds of its operational success had been sown. It was no wonder that the new railroad was predicted to be a permanent drain on the treasury by those who did not perceive either the nature of the problem or the inevitability of the solution. Conrail was popularly labeled an albatross around the neck of the taxpayer that, because of its status as a public utility, would put the U.S. government permanently into the rail business. The enemies of federal involvement predicted another U.S. Post Office. Though they had lost the battle of Conrail's startup, they sat back to await their eventual victory in its demise and perhaps were readying themselves to pick up the desirable parts of the carcass.

Conrail confounded them. In the ensuing years, the government invested $7 billion in Conrail, which took advantage of its quasi-nationalized status to produce surprisingly quick results. Approximately half of that sum went for plant rehabilitation and rebuilt or new rolling stock. The rest went for severance pay to the vast numbers of employees who were permanently furloughed and to cover operating losses. Conrail also successfully shed itself of the last vestiges of its commuter services by 1982. They were spun off to Amtrak by legislation (to be discussed in the section on Amtrak that follows).

In its first nine months of operation (April through December 1976) the Consolidated Rail Corporation lost $205,453,000 — less than the estimated $295,000,000 loss projected in the final system plan. This was done with operating revenues of $2,447,292,000 and operating and other expenses adding up to $2,652,745,000. The new system handled 73.4 billion revenue ton-miles of traffic on over 34,000 track miles (17,000 route miles) covering sixteen states and the District of Columbia. In this period, Conrail used $484,000,000 from an initial $2,026,000,000 rehabilitation authorization appropriated for its first four years. (The Final System Plan's original projection, incidentally, was $696,000,000 for the 1976 period.) This investment paid for the installation of 727 miles of new rail and 4,550,000 new crossties as well as the heavy repair of rolling stock. Eleven thousand, nine hundred twenty cars and 779 locomotives were rehabilitated, 13.7 percent over the projected goal of 11,159 and 625, respectively. Eight thousand, two hundred sixty miles of existing track structures were also upgraded to eliminate delays, resulting in the lifting of 7,791 miles in slow orders (lowered speed limits due to bad track) during 1976, allowing faster and more reliable service.

These figures illustrate both the magnitude of the deferred maintenance Conrail inherited and how quickly the physical turnaround began. Profits projected for 1979 would not be realized until 1981, though. In its first nine months, Conrail operated an average of 1,500 freight trains daily and carried an average of 360,000 commuters each business day in 1,864 commuter trains. The installation of nineteen high-speed data inquiry units allowed more efficient response to the 8,000 daily customer inquiries about rates, whereabouts of shipments, and so on. This was a critical factor in building shipper confidence. New marketing initiatives to go after business previously lost to trucks were planned and put into place in this period, copying what other non-rail-transportation marketers had been doing all long.[39]

During startup, labor unions representing Conrail's 99,827 employees displayed a remarkable degree of cooperation, particularly in light of the prospects of rapidly shrinking memberships and the unpalatable but unavoidable need to give major concessions on productivity and pay issues. They negotiated many new work rules that greatly improved productivity (joining with the substantial productivity improvements made possible by physical rehabilitation), and they agreed to pay scales below the industry norm in return for 15 percent ownership in the new entity. Thus, Conrail's startup was assisted significantly by labor's realistic view. If labor had failed to cooperate, costly work stoppages and deliberate inefficiencies could have destroyed the railroad.

In spite of the fact that Conrail was designed in a hurry and the Nixon administration had staffed the U.S.R.A. with key policy people who were not fully committed to either the viability of rail transport or the appropriateness of a federal role in it, Conrail's development went forward. It was not a miracle, as some have called it; it was the result of a soundly conceived structure and implementation of well-developed plans by competent professional railroaders who had the necessary support of public-policy-makers.

Once the startup period passed, Conrail management relearned the art of marketing. By the 1970s, the art had virtually disappeared from heavily regulated railroads with a large percentage of captive shippers. Conrail sharpened its marketing skills to compete with other modes of transportation, thereby bringing some new, noncaptive business back to its rails. The system finally got excellent management by promoting experienced people from within and by hiring L. Stanley Crane to take charge. Crane, newly rehired from Southern Railway (because of retirement-age policy) had a deserved reputation as a tough but competent railroader.

As the rapid physical rehabilitation began to allow competitive performance, Crane and his new team went to work. They introduced articulated container-on-flat-car platforms, which were cheaper to operate and which allowed the railroad to compete with trucks more effectively. They also introduced cabooseless trains with smaller crews, made possible by labor agreements. State-of-the-art locomotives were purchased from General Motors and General Electric, and older, less efficient locomotives were sold at a good price. Redundant trackage capacity was shed, and extensive centralized traffic control equipment was installed to automate dispatching and make existing trackage capacity higher. All of these improvements had their effects: Conrail went from a railroad that posted a loss of $1 million a day in its first year to a 1984 profit of approximately $1.3 million a day, with almost $1 billion in cash reserves.[40] It also delivered on-time transportation regularly rather than occasionally, and loss and damage claims by shippers dropped dramatically.

The dimensions of the turnaround speak for themselves. Losses were $246 million in the nine months of 1976, $412 million in 1977, $430 million in 1978, $221 million in 1979, and $244 million in 1980, the year in which the Final System plan projected the first profits. In 1979, 1980, and 1981, the railroad experienced three severe and costly winters. In 1981, however, Conrail posted a net profit of $39 million. In 1982, the profit increased to $174 million. Skeptics began to take note as Conrail continued with a profit of $313 million in 1983. Progress continued in 1984 with the posting of a half billion dollars in profit. Results from 1985 and 1986 show continuing high profits at rates almost comparable to the preceding several years. Profits in 1987 and 1988 were $299 million and $306 million, respectively. Total assets grew from $3,761 million on December 31, 1976, to $7,224 million exactly twelve years later, while long-term debt increased during the same period from $1,341 million to only $850 million.

At the same time, the number of employees shrank from 99,827 (including passenger service employees) to 32,595, with no passenger employees. Route miles contracted from the original 17,000 to 13,443, covering fifteen states. Trains operated on a daily average basis declined from 1,500 to 760, with an equipment fleet of 94,000 freight cars and 2,800 locomotives, most either new or in excellent shape, equalling those of the best of its competitors.

Revenue ton-miles in 1988 totalled 78.8 billion, up from 60.8 billion in 1982, at the depth of the recession, and comparable to the 73.4 billion carried in the nine months of 1976 on the bigger system. Employee productivity gains totalled an impressive 38 percent in the period after 1982 and 45 percent after 1980. In 1988, with a stabilized work force, ton-miles increased 6.2

percent overall over 1987. Maintenance of way (track maintenance) productivity man-hours in 1984, a key track rehabilitation year, were also up from 1983, with improvements of 5.7 percent per man-hour for laying rail, 8.6 percent for installing ties, and 10.6 percent for surfacing (rehabilitation of existing track structures).

All of this had beneficial effects on service. Down time for freight cars averaged about 3 percent, and less than 8 percent of the road's diesel-electric locomotives were out of service for periodic inspection and repairs at any given time (which was among the best in the industry). On-time performance of freight trains was 86 percent in 1984 versus 32 percent in 1976 and continues at high levels as new centralized dispatching technology comes on line. Average transit time for moving loaded freight cars declined in excess of 20 percent between 1979 and 1984. Conrail's total transportation cost for moving these cars also declined 29 percent after 1980, reflecting increases both in operating efficiency and carload volume due to the modern freight car fleet. Operating costs as a percentage of revenues declined to 86.2 percent in 1984 from a respectable 90.6 percent in 1983. In 1988, they remained at 86.2 percent.

Reflecting these new efficiencies, fuel use declined 12 percent from 1982 to 1985, and cash on hand rose from $151 million in 1978 to $846 million in 1984 with $666 million on hand in 1988. Conrail became the largest volume piggyback carrier in the United States and pioneered in the acquisition of a variety of new equipment to further improve productivity in this area. Conrail was a rolling test bed for piggyback service.[41]

The net result is that the quasi-nationalized Consolidated Rail Corporation was a vastly more efficient railroad than its private predecessors. It experienced a massive financial renaissance and improved service while simultaneously improving employee productivity by equally great margins. In the post-Staggers environment of the 1980s, Conrail not only met and made gains on the long-haul truck competition but also met the competition of other profitable private railroads operating in the same environment and did so without drawing on federal funds after mid-1981. The railroad sold to private interests in 1987 was a far cry from the sad legacy of the Penn Central.

While this turnaround was remarkable, particularly because

it happened in the environment of high fuel costs, foreign competition, unusually bad (expensive) weather, and the continuing Northeast-Midwest heavy industry depression and general economic recession, it did not take place in a vacuum. It could not have happened without an end to punishing economic regulation. The Staggers Act constituted the break that Conrail needed, providing long-overdue partial deregulation of all U.S. railroads. Pushed through by the Carter administration, it gave the ailing U.S. rail industry the freedom to compete more fairly with trucks. Conrail's Crane, aware of what the Staggers Act would do for his charge, was one of the major advocates for its passage. In his congressional testimony, he predicted that it would save Conrail. Staggers allowed Conrail's new state-of-the-art systems to compete aggressively in the marketplace and to attract needed sources of private capital. The Philadelphia giant outstripped many other profitable railroads in performance improvement under Staggers and began to act very much like a private business instead of a quasi-nationalized one during this period.

Conrail's days as a quasi-nationalized railroad were numbered, however. The Northeast Rail Services Act of 1981, pushed through during the hectic legislative period of budget reconciliation, mandated its eventual return to the private sector of the political economy. The 1981 act was championed by Reagan and his conservative majority and was designed to reverse the policy of quasi-nationalization. At the same time, the Reagan administration attempted to defund Amtrak completely.

The law mandated that the Department of Transportation sell the federal government's interest in Conrail to the private sector just as it began to earn a profit and repay its debt. It expressed a preference that the entire system be disposed of as a single entity if certain profitability tests were reached. The act did not require the sale to be promulgated by a certain date. However, it was a clear signal that a 1981 majority of federal policymakers desired to return at least partially to an earlier era of rail policy as usual. It set into motion the chain of events that led to the 1987 privatization of Conrail.

After the United States Railway Association (the agency set up to create Conrail, not to be confused with the United States

Railroad Administration of World War I) certified that Conrail was legally profitable under the terms of the act, the Department of Transportation advertised for bids for purchase of Conrail. By the deadline for receipt of bids, fifteen offers had been received, ranging from "$5.00 and certain other considerations" to nearly $2 billion.

The Department of Transportation specified that it was looking for the bidder that would leave Conrail in the strongest financial condition after the sale, best protect service patterns, and give maximum return to the federal taxpayers consistent with the other objectives.[42] This was widely interpreted to be a move to pave the way for the bid of the Norfolk Southern Railroad. Secretary of Transportation Dole announced that she intended to recommend to Congress that the NS bid of $1.2 billion be accepted in spite of the fact that the Conrail management had put in a bid of identical worth via a package of stock for sale to the public (administered by the Morgan-Stanley investment firm), which would preserve competition by leaving Conrail independent and competing with Norfolk Southern and CSX in its territory.

The sale was duly considered by Congress, with the Norfolk Southern proposal and the Morgan-Stanley proposal (publicly supported by Conrail's management) being the two realistic contenders, in spite of Reagan administration opposition to the latter. The Senate eventually passed the Norfolk Southern sale, but the House did not, effectively killing the sale in 1986. There were many in the House who favored a de facto continuation of quasi-nationalization. That could have been effectively promulgated by doing nothing, allowing the federal government to continue to reap Conrail's profits. The impending privatization cast a heavy operational shadow on Conrail's management, consuming its time and attentions and affecting its policies during a critical period in its history. Conrail was privatized by a stock sale in March 1987 and has continued to operate profitably to date.

The post-privatization Consolidated Rail Corporation is a large, investor-owned, for-profit freight railroad. It is a relatively major corporation, the principal product of which is hauling goods by rail. Thus, it is not as diversified as many of its competitors. Because of its size and history, it remains a major actor in the political economy of the United States, privatization notwithstanding.

Based in Philadelphia, Pennsylvania, Conrail provides rail freight service to fifteen states and the District of Columbia.[43] Its past and present employees still own about 15 percent of its stock (approximately 10.4 million shares), which was distributed on October 1, 1987, when the ESOP was abolished under terms of the privatization legislation.[45]

The Pennsylvania Railroad once called itself "the standard railroad of the world," which was part advertising hype and part truth. Though Conrail makes no such claim, it is reasonable to label it a worthy heir of that tradition (at least in the North American world) due to its size, its many state-of-the-art innovations in physical plant, its widespread use of common products of the railway supply industry, its relatively efficient operating procedures, its mostly modern work rules, and its phoenixlike resurrection from the wreckage of the bankruptcies of the Penn Central, Reading, Lehigh Valley, Central of New Jersey, Erie-Lackawanna, and Lehigh and Hudson River railroads under the terms of the Staggers Act. Close examination of the Consolidated Rail Corporation as an operating and financial entity helps us to grasp its size in relative scale, giving us insight into the magnitude of its creation, development, and privatization by Washington. This examination also allows us to compare it to other, similar transportation entities.

At the end of 1985, Conrail had approximately 33,000 employees, down from the 99,000 inherited from its bankrupt predecessors in 1976.[44] About 45,000 railroaders worked for the Union Pacific, 48,000 in transportation service for CSX, and 38,000 for Norfolk Southern in 1985. These three railroads are private Conrail competitors of roughly equal size. Norfolk Southern and CSX both have extensive operations in the same general service area as Conrail. In the same year, the Soo Line had 3,713 employees. The Soo Line is a relatively small midwestern Class I (major) railroad. While it is dwarfed by Conrail, it is much bigger than the many short lines now proliferating in American railroading. It is smaller today than it was in 1985 due to several short-line spin-offs.

Most Conrail employees are unionized and follow traditional rail craft lines and jurisdictions. Even though current collective bargaining agreements call for small crews and a diminished work force, the railroad enjoys a good deal of employee loyalty. This aided its return to profitability and surely continues to have a beneficial effect, judging by productivity figures and the attitudes encountered by this analyst during interviews. Given its successful long-term pattern of cooperative negotiations with the United Transportation Workers, the Brotherhood of Locomotive Engineers, the Brotherhood of Railway and Airline Clerks, and other major rail trade unions, Conrail has to be judged successful here. It is probable that this will continue in the immediate future, since there is nothing on the horizon that appears to threaten good labor relations.

Conrail in its last quasi-nationalized year had about $3.3 billion in annual sales for transportation services.[46] According to annual report data, this revenue figure was almost exactly the average of the Norfolk Southern's performance, less than CSX's recent $4.8 billion, and slightly less than Union Pacific's $3.8 billion. Conrail had approximately $1 billion in cash reserves and generated a net profit of $500 million in 1984, slightly less in 1985, and $431 million in 1986; 1987 and 1988 figures ($299 million and $306 million, respectively) were substantially lower because of the privatization-mandated loss of tax offsets from previous losses. (Because it earned profits only for the last seven years, after five years of losses, the railroad paid no federal corporate income taxes before 1987.) This compares to a $430 million Conrail net loss in 1978, and 1984 net profits for Union Pacific of $494 million, for CSX of $657, and for Norfolk Southern of $482 million, and a net loss for Amtrak in the same period of $763 million. All of these railroads earned slightly less in 1985 (except CSX, which took a loss due to a write-down associated with restructuring and accounting changes) as the general rail economy softened. Figures from 1986-88 show similar patterns.

The Consolidated Rail Corporation has a chairman and chief executive officer, and vice presidents of Finance and Administration, Public Affairs, Governmental Affairs, and Law, and their subordinates who answer directly to the top.[47] The railroad also has a president and chief operating officer. The vice president of Marketing and Sales, and the president of Penn Truck Lines, the senior vice president of Operations, and vice presidents of Labor Relations, Resource Development, and

Materials and Purchasing answer to the president. This structure resembles that of the analogous railroads mentioned above as well as those of the rest of the industry. It did not change significantly after privatization, although 1989 saw further streamlining at the middle levels.

The Philadelphia Conrail executive staff manages current (1988 year end) assets total approximately $7.25 billion. Norfolk Southern had about $1 billion more, Union Pacific about $10.4 billion, Conrail about $6.2 billion in 1984, the key year. CSX asset figures are not analogous because they include too much nonrail activity in the $11.5 billion total.[48]

Like the post-1981 quasi-nationalized Conrail, the private Conrail no longer receives federal subsidies. It reinvests from profits and borrowings like its competitors. While Conrail has generated a net profit since 1981, the approximately $7 billion of public investment Conrail received from 1976 through 1980 still has a beneficial asset effect that contributes to its profitability, even though part had been repaid before privatization. Without those public funds, resurrection of the railroad could not have taken place, and it would not have been a salable property.

The present Conrail is quite different from foreign government-owned railroads, though it is not very different from its immediate preprivatization self. Nationalized railroads in Europe and Japan, for example, have many more employees, fewer route miles (though more track miles), and many more trains.[49] They are predominantly in the business of carrying passengers and subsidized freight to socially dictated rather than economically dictated locations. Because of this, they have substantially worse financial results, requiring vast subsidies and provoking periodic calls for cutbacks to lower deficits.

Before divestiture, Conrail was technically a government agency, though it did not function like one due to its status as a quasi-national entity.[50] However, even if it had been fully public, a comparison of the pre-1987 railroad with giant federal agencies like the Department of Defense or the Department of Health and Human Services demonstrates Conrail's relatively small presence. It operated in only fifteen states, had many fewer employees, and had a much smaller annual budget (Defense operates at around $350 billion, compared to Conrail's $3.3 billion.) Running a railroad simply involves many fewer tasks than defending the global interests of a superpower or administering a national health and welfare system.

Relative to other American investor-owned railroads, however, Conrail is one of the industry majors, as comparisons to Union Pacific, CSX, and Norfolk Southern demonstrate. Conrail is one of the "big seven" rail systems that are presently operating in the wake of the merger movement that has swept U.S. railroading in the last generation (presuming the I.C.C.-disallowed Santa Fe-Southern Pacific consolidation is not resurrected in the future). While a true transcontinental railroad has not yet emerged in the United States, the merger movement has left three eastern and four western rail systems of vast proportions. It has also left an ever-proliferating coterie of small regional and short-line railroads, currently numbering about five hundred. They range in size from relatively significant regionals like the Soo and the Wisconsin Central (which operates almost 2,000 miles of former Soo Line track) to some tiny properties with a few miles of track and one locomotive. Conrail remains a very important railroad, able to compete with the other principal Class I's and dwarfing all other railroads.

On an operating basis, Conrail is similar to the other six U.S. rail giants. As a result of its aggressive capital improvements program, Conrail is a major customer of the rail supply industry, buying new, state-of-the-art communications and signal equipment, locomotives, freight cars, track equipment, rails, and cross ties. As it serves the major cities and industrial belts of the northeastern quadrant of the United States, Conrail acts as a hauler of raw materials and finished goods in both eastward and westward directions, from St. Louis and Chicago to the port cities of the Great Lakes and the East Coast. Like most large railroads, Conrail faces special and expensive geographical problems. Its main operational hurdles are the Allegheny Mountains and the fierce winters in the Great Lakes area.

Because of the declining industrial base (particularly in steel and automobiles) of the still-populous East, Conrail's traffic is slightly unbalanced, with more goods coming eastward and more empty freight cars going westward for reloading. It is heavily dependent upon coal, steel products, and automobiles for its traffic base, and the amount of these commodities shipped on Conrail has fluctuated with the fortunes of their shippers. Recently, Conrail's aggressive marketing, made possible by deregulation, has rectified this somewhat, especially in the trailer and container hauling business in which Conrail excels. Conrail potentially serves the source of nearly half of the U.S. industrial potential. It handles 15 percent of all U.S. rail shipments via its seven hundred trains per day.

The Consolidated Rail Corporation is represented in Washington, D.C., by much more than the few miles of track within sight of the capitol. The railroad has maintained a high-profile Washington presence since its origins in the public policy process. Its fifteen-state service area incorporates the districts of many important members in both parties of both houses of Congress, giving the railroad important congressional clout. Key members who have gone to bat for Conrail include Senator Heinz of Pennsylvania, a Republican who voted against the Reagan Administration on the proposed sale to Norfolk Southern, and Representatives James Florio of New Jersey and John Dingell of Michigan, both important Democrats who control the flow of rail legislation in the House of Representatives.

The White House had paid close attention to Conrail as a federal property and to its potential salability to the private sector from the time of Conrail's creation until the privatization. Its progress as an investor-owned firm is presumably still a matter of federal interest, given the consequences of its failure. Thus, a privatized Conrail would be important in Washington even if the railroad were not as adept as it is at public policy advocacy. In this respect, Conrail has always behaved more like a private corporation than a federal agency. Chief Executive Officer Stanley Crane has, from his appointment, been a frequent visitor to Capitol Hill. In pre-privatization days, he was treated more like a visiting corporate executive than the head of a federal agency. The railroad has also hired professional lobbyists to plead its case from time to time. Given its legislative successes, Conrail clearly maintains the ear of Congress. The railroad essentially controlled its own destiny via successful lobbying on legislation concerning its return to the private sector, outmaneuvering the Reagan White House in the process. It also had a significant positive effect on the passage of the Staggers Act of 1980, which benefited the whole railroad industry. Presumably, the railroad stands ready and able to intervene effectively in the rail policy climate of the future as it deems necessary.

To place the transition from public to private railroad into perspective, it is important to recall that Conrail was never fully nationalized. Before March 1987, it was quasi-nationalized[51] (like Amtrak and unlike most foreign railroads except Japan's). The railroad was owned by the government but allowed (even encouraged) to operate with the managerial and market freedom of a private corporation. In fact if not in law, public policy did not set routes and rates. Instead, they were set by Conrail's balance sheet, the competitive environment, and managerial judgment. Thus, Consolidated Rail operated like a private, for-profit corporation throughout its history, in spite of its ownership. This made the transition to private ownership easier (avoiding some of the problems British Telecom has experienced) and created a more comfortable stance for policy-makers, allowing them to more closely associate their policies with the culture of the political economy.

Conrail received much attention from the public, the government, its shippers, and the press because it played two unprecedented roles within eleven years in the political economy of the United States. First, it was called upon to resurrect vital rail service to the Northeast and Midwest and made a profit doing it where many others had failed for a long time. Then it became the largest new equity offering and the largest privatization in U.S. history. Its role as a creation and an instrument of public policy and as a business firm has undergone rapid transformation. Clearly, the future of Conrail and U.S. public rail policy holds further transitions, a theme we will return to in the last two chapters.

The National Railroad Passenger Corporation

According to Amtrak, "[it] began operation on May 1, 1971, with a $40 million appropriation from Congress, a handful of employees, cast-off passenger cars from the private railroads, and no track or maintenance facilities of its own. Amtrak's mandate: To breathe life into a dying rail passenger service that the railroads had been unable to save. Few people gave Amtrak much chance to survive the two years for which it was originally funded."[52]

Amtrak was correct. By the time Congress created the National Railroad Passenger Corporation as a quasi-public, government-financed, profit-seeking corporation in 1970,[53] rail passenger service in the United States had declined precipitously, and passenger service deficits of the railroads had risen to alarming proportions. Policymakers' answer, originally called Railpax and designed to be more quasi-private than quasi-public,[54] was the National Railroad Passenger Corporation, known as Amtrak. Like Conrail, it marked a major rail policy departure for the U.S. government.

In its heyday in the 1920s, American rail passenger service was the standard for the world. The modern equipment, elegant on-board service, and reliable and extensive schedules were an impressive achievement for the nation's private railroads. In 1929, U.S. Class I railroads had 226,703 miles of tracks in passenger service and hauled 47,797 passenger cars over them.[55]

Changes in transportation technology, public policy, and railroad managements all took their toll. By 1966, the Class I railroads were operating only 11,687 passenger cars over 72,796 miles of railroad.[56] In that year, the railroads chalked up 165,498,000 passenger train-miles, 18.11 percent less than the previous year. Compare this to 382,313,000 passenger train miles in 1949 in the height of the postwar campaigns by some railroads to resurrect passenger service. Passenger train miles declined each year from 1949 until Amtrak's start-up.[57]

From 1949 until Amtrak, passenger service deficits for Class I railroads vacillated, ranging from $380 to $723 million, and from around 20 percent to nearly 49 percent of net freight revenue for the period (although the general trend was downward as passenger train miles declined).[58] The exact deficit is controversial, however. Lynn writes, for example, "The passenger-service deficit, so-called, is and always has been a statistical mirage; a fraud ... due to I.C.C. formulae [requiring railroads to file separate statements of expenses charged to freight and passengers] adopted in 1887, retired in 1894 after attack, but revived and revised in 1949.... [It] allowed millions in maintenance and overhead which would need to be paid anyway. It was opposed by the New York Stock Exchange, the Post Office, the City of Philadelphia, and others."[59]

U.S. rail passenger service was a money losing proposition overall by the 1950s. The losses continued to accelerate until I.C.C.-granted train-off petitions began to reduce them in absolute terms. Some trains undoubtedly were profitable during the entire period, of course, but the aggregate service was not. This parallels similar financial results in Europe and elsewhere. Passengers simply cost more to haul than freight, and the revenues cannot make up for all of the cost.

What nearly killed the American passenger train? Technology, public policy, and railroad managements have been suggested as the culprits. The modern highway and airway networks became practical only after the invention and perfection of the private automobile and the airliner. Once perfected, they became affordable and, in some ways, preferable alternatives to the passenger train. Thus, technology contributed to the passenger train's decline. But it was not wholly responsible.

The decisions by the United States government to build the interstate highway system and to create the extensive airways and airports system (including massive subsidies) contributed to the appeal and practicality of automobiles and airlines and made them viable commercial competitors to the passenger train by the 1950s. Another frequently cited contributing factor was the decision by the U.S. Post Office to cancel passenger train mail contracts. Most trains were carrying far more mail and express than passengers. Lynn, however, argues otherwise. In his analysis of 306 ICC 417, he quotes the ICC as saying that Post Office cancellation of mail contracts was not responsible for the demise of the passenger train. In fact, the opposite was true. The Post Office said, "From February 1, 1953, to December 31, 1966, a total of 2,578 mail carrying passenger trains had been discontinued after their mail traffic had been removed at the request of the railroads, and 798 were discontinued after their mail traffic had been removed at the initiative of the Post Office."[60]

Railroads themselves contributed to the decline of passenger trains. They failed to stick with promotional efforts long enough and executed many of them half-heartedly, presumably because freight service was more lucrative and because they were not adept at marketing, despite some serious efforts. Individual firms differed on their support of passenger trains in the postwar years. Some, like the Atlantic Coast Line, the Seaboard, the Illinois Central, the Great Northern, the Northern Pacific, the Burlington (C.B. & Q.), the Union Pacific, and the Santa Fe (A. T. & S.F.) invested heavily in expensive streamlined equipment and promoted passenger service quite vigorously into the mid-1950s, though to a much lesser extent than airlines. Unfortunately, there were few market studies done, so that even pro-passenger railroads knew little about their customers. Others, particularly eastern carriers like the Pennsylvania and the New York Central, made lesser efforts for a shorter period of time. Soon after World War II, they commenced a spiral of raising fares and cutting service in the hopes of driving passengers away, thereby giving their train-off petitions to the I.C.C. increased credibility.[61]

Thus, for a variety of reasons, the passenger train was in serious decline by the 1960s, in spite of its high social utility and the political visibility of trains that caused policymakers to fight for them in hopes of avoiding a public opinion backlash. As the crisis deepened, the government was forced to act. One of the first actions was the Pell Plan, first advocated by the Rhode Island Senator in 1962, to create an eight-state authority for high-speed rail passenger service along the northeastern coast. This eventually became the federal government's Northeastern Corridor Project, which brought technologically sophisticated, high-speed rail service to the heavily traveled route between Boston and Washington. It even got the support of the by-then antipassenger Pennsylvania Railroad, the owner of most of the line. This line is now owned by Amtrak and is the carrier's fastest and most lucrative operation.

At the 1965 signing of the Pell legislation, President Johnson asked railroad executives to reconsider the decline of passenger service generally and report back to him in three months. Their January 1966 report was a poorly conceived and researched document, which was dismissed by the White House. At the same time, the Canadian National Railroad started their Rapido service between Toronto and Montreal, using conventional equipment and beating the analogous New York Central Cleveland-Chicago service by 50 percent in fares and a full hour in time.[62] (The Japanese Shinkansen line takes three hours to go the same distance, the CN five hours, the New York Central six hours.) These events added pressure for governmental intervention.

Professor George Hilton argues that Amtrak legislation stemmed from the false perception of policymakers that railroad managers killed the passenger train by driving away passengers. He believed its true killer was competition from other, subsidized transport modes.[63] Weaver, on the other hand, refuted that by showing that "most executive policymakers were aware (although many legislators probably were not) that the establishment of a new organization would not be sufficient to make rail passenger service profitable again. They nevertheless supported Amtrak as a means to further their own policy goals."[64] These goals presumably included perceptions of the role that the passenger train served in the public interest of the nation.

The legislative struggle to create a national railroad passenger authority began in the 1960s and culminated in the quasi-nationalization of U.S. rail passenger service in 1970. According to economist Lloyd Musolf, Congress had already decided that government intervention was necessary and questioned only what form it would take. The Department of Transportation offered Congress three different proposals: federal aid to public agencies willing to subsidize railroad passenger service; a government-chartered private corporation called Railpax to provide core service and to be jointly owned by the railroads and the public; and provision of federal grants for improvements to profitable service areas or to local governments to cover operating deficits. The DOT favored Railpax because "no federal funds would be required."[65]

As the policy battles heated up, the railroads proved to be uninterested in investment in Railpax. However, the Nixon administration sided with that alternative in 1970. Arguments, reports, and compromises mounted, finally leading to passage of the Rail Passenger Service Act of 1970, which created what is now called Amtrak. The statute called for "a for-profit corporation" that would operate a "basic system."[66]

As Musolf puts it, "Most members of Congress would probably have agreed with [DOT] Secretary Volpe that 'the corporation will be like any other corporation. It will either flounder on the rocks because it provides poor service or it will prosper because it provides a better mousetrap.'"[67] The corporation did not flounder on the rocks in spite of mounting and permanent deficits that contributed to poor service in the initial years.

By 1972, to forestall Amtrak's bankruptcy and the cessation of politically valued service, Congress was forced to grant $325 million in additional appropriations and loan guarantees and increased its hold over Amtrak, effectively bringing it closer to quasi-nationalization. In 1976, Amtrak was given the Northeast Corridor route (Boston to Washington, Philadelphia to Harrisburg) as part of Conrail's creation and continued to attract more and more public funds to make up for deficits and to fund capital improvements that would allow better service.

According to Weaver, with the passage of The Amtrak Improvement Act of 1978, Congress "formally recognized that Amtrak would probably never be profitable. Instead, the company had become a ward of the federal government.... The Omnibus Reconciliation Act of 1981 eliminated most of the vestiges of Amtrak's quasi-private status by issuing preferred stock to the Secretary of Transportation in recognition of DOT investment in the company and by eliminating railway (common stock) representatives from Amtrak's Board of Directors. It is impossible, however, to pinpoint ... a decision to nationalize Amtrak.... Congress and the executive failed to point Amtrak ... with a clear and consistent mandate; instead, they pushed Amtrak through ... compromise measures."[68] In Musolf's words, "By adding 'operated and managed as' in front of 'a for-profit corporation,' a reasonable statutory compromise was reached."[69] Thus, the powerful effects of the culture of the U.S. political economy were manifested in Amtrak's for-profit status. Their manifestation continued in policymakers' reluctance to modify Amtrak into a quasi-nationalized railroad in spite of the fiscal realities of rail passenger service in contemporary America. The policy legacy of all this was a hybrid, a not quite public and not quite private quasi-nationalization of rail passenger service, which combined symbols with concessions to reality.

Amtrak's accomplishments have been significant since 1971,

although the corporation has not been without its share of problems. Today, it appears that its quasi-nationalization is a permanent feature of the near future of U.S. railroading. Amtrak is unlikely to follow Conrail into privatization, thus insuring the continuing direct presence of the U.S. government in the rail political economy.

On its first day of service on May 1, 1971, Amtrak had eight federally appointed incorporators (later to become directors) and a chief executive (Roger Lewis). Court challenges to its initiation had been turned aside. Train miles went from 63 million to 24 million and route miles from 43,000 to 16,000.[70] Due to inheritance of outmoded and worn-out equipment, maintenance of nationally wandering equipment by individual railroad personnel not familiar with it, an Arab oil boycott that hit in 1973 before Amtrak could efficiently handle a traffic surge, failure to purchase new, reliable equipment in a timely fashion, poor route planning,[71] and mounting deficits, Amtrak's problems increased. Service ranged from acceptable to wretched.

Nevertheless, Amtrak grew and began to deal with its problems. Its public image slowly improved. States began to subsidize desired Amtrak services under section 403(b) of the original enabling legislation for the N.R.P.C., thus helping Amtrak maintain service and public image.[72] By 1975, passenger train miles had climbed to 30 million, a figure maintained in 1985, with fluctuations in between. Route miles currently total 24,000.[73]

Financial performance has continued to improve, going from a .58 revenue to expense ratio in Fiscal Year 1985 to .69 in Fiscal Year 1988. Passenger miles have climbed over the 5.6 billion mark, traffic density continues to improve, and ratios of both revenue to short- and long-term avoidable costs have improved. Still, the N.R.P.C. received $587 million in federal subsidies in fiscal 1986, which has declined since to $574 million in 1988. Operating subsidies have declined slightly since 1983 (in constant FY88 dollars), and passenger miles per dollar of federal support have increased slightly as well, to over nine in 1988.[74] Contributing to this increased performance were the rising costs of automobile travel due to foreign energy costs, the ability of Amtrak to control its own Northeastern Corridor, and new union agreements that allowed the line to employ its own crews under a day's pay instead of a mileage contract, thereby improving cost performance on board the trains.

Nevertheless, problems persist. Passenger traffic has not returned to even the depressed 1970 levels, due in part to the loss of a national network of feeder lines. Amtrak has also had to constantly defend its appropriations on Capitol Hill as the Reagan administration sought to defund and/or cut it back repeatedly, albeit with only limited success. Today (1988 figures are the last full ones available), the quasi-nationalized railroad takes in $1.11 billion in revenues, has operating expenses of $1.76 billion, and serves 21.5 million intercity riders and 15.4 million commuters under state and local subsidized commuter service. It has 298 locomotives that average ten years in age, and owns and leases 1,853 passenger cars with an average age of 16.6 years. Its new computerized reservations system has been put on line, tying it with travel agency and airline systems more effectively than before. The railroad has also begun to solicit small-package freight business and has rented its rights-of-way for fiber optics installations in an effort to bring in additional revenue. The Boston-Washington route has been almost completely brought up to state-of-the-art roadbed and automated traffic control standards, allowing 125 mph speeds in regular service (compared to French TGV speeds of 160 mph). Its stations have been modernized (many are new and much smaller than those they replaced, appropriate to current needs), and its on-time service is fair (71 percent — actually declining slightly in recent years because of ageing equipment), while its on-train service ranges from good to very good in comparison with comparable Canadian and European service. Class I American railroads took in approximately twenty-six times the total operating freight revenues of Amtrak in 1985, with a net loss for Amtrak compared to modest average profits for the freight railroads.[75] In the twelve months ending September 30, 1986, Amtrak was seventh on a top-ten ranking of Amtrak and the largest scheduled domestic air carriers in the United States.

In summary, Amtrak must be judged a success. It has provided the nation with limited but competent rail passenger service in the public interest. It also has acquired a corporate stability and level of political backing[76] that should merit future public policy support despite large federal budget deficits looming in the 1990s and the precedent of the privatization of Conrail. Although the pro-private culture of the U.S. political economy still exerts a powerful influence, the fact that Amtrak is not profitable and is not likely to be so on a long-term basis coupled with the continuing need for rail service allows us to predict that policymakers will not tamper with Amtrak. Whether by accident or design, the federal government made reasonably correct policy choices over the long run as it first created and then gradually quasi-nationalized Amtrak. Given the alternatives of unpopular nationalization and doomed-to-fail privatization, the policies still make sense.

Rail Deregulation

Beyond the quasi-nationalizations of Amtrak and Conrail and the privatization of Conrail, the other recent major federal policy initiative into the political economy of railroading has been the partial deregulation of railroads. This policy's principal beneficiaries have been the private railroads (because they are so numerous), but it applies to all railroads, public and private. This initiative has been responsible for an important renaissance of U.S. railroads in the twentieth century: its impact on them rivals that of the two world wars.

The principal component of partial deregulation was the Staggers Rail Act of 1980. Administrative regulations of the Interstate Commerce Commission, other statutes, court decisions, and the general movement toward partial deregulation in the political economy of the last generation also contributed to this "remarkable series of events"[77] of the 1970s. The contemporary public policy of partial deregulation (not all regulations have or were contemplated to be removed) embodies cancellation of the majority of regulations of rail prices and service levels. General economic regulatory authority outside of a "zone of reasonableness" remains, just as do environmental and safety regulations.

The history of partial deregulation of American railroads is virtually the history of railroads themselves. Railroads grew rapidly in the aftermath of the Civil War, spurred by $1.3 billion in state and federal subsidies. In Moore's view, this rapidly led to redundancy of overcapacity and cutthroat competition, which "forced" railroads into cartels and predatory price behavior.[78] This was, of course, the "robber baron era." It brought governmental retaliation against the railroads, as interest groups clamored for the creation of strong federal regulation. This movement of Grangers, Progressives, some railroads,[79] shippers, and elected officials culminated in the creation of the Interstate Commerce Commission in 1887. These groups demanded and got federal action modeled on previously existing but ineffectual state regulation of railroad monopolies.

The early I.C.C. was also ineffectual. By the first decade of the twentieth century, however, strong economic regulation of railroads became the national policy norm. By 1920, regulation's negative effect was noted in national policy, and a fair return for rail carriers was also legislated, as were rationalization plans for railroads. These countercyclical policies failed because railroads had declined too far for nondirect, limited measures to be effective. The weight of I.C.C. regulation, the competitive pressures from newly emerging, subsidized transportation modes, and heavy railroad usage brought about by World War I had depressed railroads seriously enough to require sweeping policy changes for amelioration. Defensive efforts by the railroads to extend regulation to other modes eventually succeeded with the passage of the 1935 Motor Carrier Act[80] and later regulations of commercial air transportation. However, none of these public policies were effective in restoring financial health to the rails. And none of the competing modes was economically regulated as extensively as the railroads.

This regulatory policy remained essentially intact until the 1970s, in spite of unsuccessful attempts by the Kennedy administration in 1962 to lessen surface transportation regulatory levels.[81] An active movement in the late 1950s in both Canada and the United States to partially deregulate transportation was successful by 1961 in Canada (with the MacPherson Commission Report). It failed to gather momentum in the United States because of differences in "the timing of rail industry financial crises, the distributions of costs and benefits of a policy shift, and the capability of governmental institutions to compel change."[82]

The bankruptcies of the Penn Central and other U.S. railroads, however, and the threat of cessation of railroad service to parts of the nation that led to Conrail also led the U.S. government to consider pruning economic regulation for all railroads. The crisis was too deep for policymakers to continue to defer it with palliatives. But even as relief was contemplated, shipper interests and both the Ford and Carter administrations "demanded that the antitrust immunity granted to railroad rate bureaus be substantially weakened in any move toward deregulation. As in Canada, much of the debate revolved around the question of how to protect captive shippers."[83] The interests of the railroads were only part of the equation from the point of view of policymakers.

The Railroad Revitalization and Regulatory Reform Act of 1976 granted partial relief. Ford made regulatory reform a trade-off for his support of Conrail, convincing a reluctant Congress to act in the face of bankruptcy of 21 percent of the nation's rail system, a rate of return on investment that averaged less than 2 percent, and 47,000 miles of track operable only at reduced speeds because of deterioration.[84] Unfortunately, this tepid act, which stripped the I.C.C. of power over maximum rates unless a railroad could be shown to have market dominance and demanded the I.C.C. take into account adequacy of revenues to railroads, was ineffective (mostly due to I.C.C. foot-dragging and failure of other policymakers to pursue the issue).[85]

The logjam broke in 1978-79 after the passage of an airline deregulation bill and the Carter appointment of several pro-deregulation I.C.C. commissioners and Civil Aeronautics Board members. Two years later, many of the administrative deregulations enacted by Carter's appointees were incorporated into the landmark Staggers Rail Act of 1980. Since then, the I.C.C. under both Carter and Reagan has supported deregulation and has been liberal with mergers, like the Norfolk and Western-Southern combination, until it stopped the Santa Fe–Southern Pacific merger in 1987 on anticompetitive grounds.

The Staggers Act presumes rail rates to be reasonable if they fall below a threshold of 180 percent of revenue to variable cost ratio. Rates above that are subject to I.C.C. review and change if there is no effective rail or nonrail competition for the rail rate in the eyes of the I.C.C. This is a more liberal policy than that in the 1976 "4R" act. Shipper contracts (short and long term) were legalized by the Staggers Act, and uneconomic branch lines became easier to abandon. These and several other minor provisions of the act have kept most interests happy (though labor initially opposed deregulation). The exceptions are the coal and electric utility groups, which continue to press for effective repeal of Staggers. To date, they have not been successful. Although a congressional subcommittee reported out a bill to seriously trim Staggers in 1987, it did not reach the floor for a vote.

The effects of the Staggers Act and subsequent administrative policies were swift, clearly testifying to the underlying economic and technological viability of rail transportation in a competitive economic environment. As Moore puts it, "Government studies and studies by independent scholars conclude that rates have declined and service quality has either improved or remained the same."[87] Rail profits have gone up (although competitive pressures from 1985 to date have lowered them somewhat), maintenance has increased, safety has improved, and some financial stability has been brought to the industry. The turnaround of Conrail was also due to Staggers, in the opinion of almost all involved.[88]

On the negative side, Staggers and the rail regulatory reform movement did not restore complete financial health to the rail industry. Staggers allowed service cuts to many shippers and "destructive competition" between railroads and other modes.[89] It also failed to address the question of subsidization equity between competing modes of freight and passenger transportation.

Nevertheless, putting the whole movement in perspective, Conrail and Amtrak are successful components of a new era of public policy toward railroads in the United States. By and large, Staggers has worked, being an effective measure that is congruent with the laissez-faire aspects of the culture of U.S. political economy. It allows maintenance of a capitalist solution, albeit enhanced by some regulation,[90] while solving the problem of failing railroads.

Alternatives to partial deregulation existed. In lieu of Staggers, federal policymakers could have subsidized railroads,

nationalized them in some form, or accepted gradual abandonment of most U.S. rail freight and passenger service, given the
reliance of Amtrak on private railroads outside of the Northeast
Corridor. None of these was acceptable, since the federal
government was not anxious to go deeper into the railroad
business. In the final analysis, regulation is ultimately a political
process involving interests operating through a complex,
difficult-to-move U.S. political system. It is safe to predict that
now that Staggers has been enacted, deregulation is likely to be
with us for the foreseeable future. Fortuitously, its benefits far
outweigh its costs.

Other Contemporary Legacies

The remaining components of contemporary rail public policy
in the United States do not together equal the significance of
any of the three major policies we have examined. They can be
lumped under the broad categories of encouragement of short
lines and what has been called "statelization" by William
Thoms.[91] Also of some significance is the continuing federal
encouragement (or at least tacit consent) to develop integrated
transportation firms.

As major (Class I) rail firms gradually contracted in size and
service due to dwindling business and the permissive climate
of rationalization generated by the regulatory reform movement, shippers and localities found themselves without the rail
service needed for economic development and large urban
areas found themselves without commuter passenger service.
Section 403(b) of the original Amtrak legislation allows states to
subsidize passenger service and many have done so. States
have taken advantage of the current policy climate, purchased
abandoned branch lines of Conrail and other railroads, and
licensed "designated operators" to operate their lines. State and
local governments have also given loan guarantees and other
assistance to short-line operators.[92]

These operators can break even or make a profit where Class I
railroads failed, because they can respond quickly to local
shipper needs, pay lower wages, use smaller crews, and operate
smaller, older locomotives. In fact, the Class I Southern Pacific

Transportation Company has begun to emulate short-line marketing successes with its "Adopt-a-Branch" program. While not strictly the result of federal policy per se, this short-line renaissance has grown out of the recent federal regulatory reform (including expedited I.C.C. approval of their start-ups), the "rail banking" program, which preserves unused but potentially vital lines, and the Conrail line rehabilitations that took place under quasi-nationalization. The new short lines have formed their own association and are an active interest group in the contemporary rail political economy. In the future, it is likely that they will be a force to be reckoned with.

Recent I.C.C. acceptance of many large rail mergers and relaxed rules about railroad acquisition of other modes of transportation (such as the Norfolk Southern acquisition of North American Van Lines and the CSX acquisition of Sea-Land container lines) may presage a tacit policy change that will allow railroads to become part of or even to form integrated transportation companies and offer truly national and international transportation service. It is possible that U.S. analogues to the Canadian National and Canadian Pacific transportation firms and the integrated nationalized transportation firms of Europe may be permitted, even encouraged, as U.S. transportation policies evolve. It is too soon to say with certainty that this will happen (especially in light of the I.C.C. disapproval of the Santa Fe–Southern Pacific merger and the subsequent Southern Pacific–Rio Grande merger which was allowed), but it is a possibility that bears watching in the immediate transportation policy future.

Historical developments and their contemporary policy legacies form the current political economy of railroading in the United States. Constituting not so much a brave new era as an evolution, they reflect a difference in rail policy emphasis that will form the basis of the remainder of the twentieth century's rail policies and will carry over into the twenty-first century.

chapter four

Policy Problems and Options in the Present and Near Future

T
O THIS POINT, WE HAVE LOOKED AT the history of the political economy of American railroading and described the legacies of government policy toward railroading. In this and the next chapter, we will evaluate public policies from the vantage point of a normative political theory and public policy science (in the manner of Herson, Dolbeare, Lowi, Brewer and deLeon, and Fowler[1]) and of a normative political economy (in the manner of Phelps, Keynes, Stiglitz, and Galbraith[2]).

Because railroads are likely to remain vital parts of the future of the political economy of the United States, policymakers must continue to decide what to do about them. Policy analysts must integrate policy prescription with description in order to recommend changes in rail policies based upon what has been learned from past and present railroading experiences. The goal is to broaden understanding of an important area of public policy and suggest at least the preliminary outlines of an agenda for future rail public policy in the United States.

This chapter moves toward prescription by specifying and evaluating the consequences of present rail public policies. It catalogues what transportation problems remain despite federal policy efforts to alleviate them, it looks at the institutional complex of public policy of transportation (especially rail) in the United States, and it develops an agenda for rail transportation policy for the near future. That agenda will be a critique of existing policies and a catalogue of what needs to be done to ensure a brighter rail future for the United States.

The final chapter will build on that catalogue by attempting to translate agenda items into practical policy options and solutions. It will concentrate on the lessons that ought to be learned from past policy successes and failures and recommend what needs to be done by policymakers to ensure that federal rail transportation policies for the near future are as good or better than those of the present and substantially better than those of the recent past.

Contemporary Rail Public Policies

It should be apparent from the preceding analysis that the 1970s and 1980s marked a partially new, incrementally different era in rail transportation public policy. Because of policy pressures generated by the crisis of widespread financial problems and imminent cessation of service, railroads in this period once again came to be viewed as essential transportation providers by many policymakers. The result was a rail political economy characterized by the emergence of prorailroad policies that stood alongside (rather than replaced) the many antirailroad policy holdovers from earlier eras.

The principal policy departures have already been described in the context of legacies of past rail policy. The first aspects of new policy were the creation of Amtrak in 1970 and Conrail in 1976. These were the first widespread direct interventions into the ownership and operation of American railroading since the U.S. Railway Administration experience with nationalization during World War I. Under this new policy, the federal government used its resources and authority as guardian of the public interest to preserve essential rail services. It enacted rail subsidies and programs that treated these quasi-nationalized railroads like a new industry. Funds were expended for their promotion and (re)development because they were perceived as appropriate transportation policy instruments that advanced the larger policy goals of the nation. Ideological precedents gave way to pressing problem solutions in the new era, at least until Conrail was privatized.

The second major component of the prorail public policy shift was the regulatory reform movement that culminated in the passage of the Staggers Rail Act of 1980. This act, along with its companion legislation and administrative policies described in the previous chapter, ushered in a more market-oriented regulatory policy for all U.S. railroads, both public or private. It was the most laissez-faire public policy toward railroading the nation had seen since the Interstate Commerce Commission began to be an effective regulatory force toward railroads around the turn of the twentieth century. This policy change finally gave effective de facto implementation to the goals of the Transportation Act of 1920, providing adequate revenue for rail carrier health. Clearly, it was a major factor in the transportation marketplace success of the federal government's new freight railroad.

Along with this, the federal government provided incentives and encouragement for state and local governments to assist ailing railroads. Many of these jurisdictions quickly took advantage of this new climate in order to assist local economic development.[3] Also in this period the federal government invested in the development of high-speed passenger rail service in the Boston-Washington corridor. These policies provided stronger railroads and more federal investment in them, whether by regulatory reform, quasi-nationalization, or vastly increased support of rail research and development, as embodied in the high-speed project and the Federal Rail Transportation Test Center in Pueblo, Colorado, now run under contract by the Association of American Railroads.

As collectively significant as these policies are, they have not repealed the political economy of the United States and its passive antirail bias. These policies can be put into perspective by examining their impacts and by laying them alongside other policies of the same era. To begin with, they did not significantly reverse the fortunes of the railroads. Rail rates of return on investment climbed in the early 1980s, leveled off, and then sank once again in the middle of the 1980s as the competitive environment encroached upon the benefits of the regulatory reform movement. The loosening of the economic straitjacket American railroads (public and private) had found themselves bound up in[4] proved to provide only partial relief.

Public policies of quasi-nationalization were not completely successful if one looks at maintenance of rail service. Though a core system of rail passenger service was maintained during this era, it was not as extensive as it had been (or as the nation needed), and it continued to be limited by low appropriations relative to need. Rail freight service was similarly maintained in the Northeast and Midwest. It, too, was cut back substantially. What remained was reliable and cost-effective, but many communities lost all or part of needed rail service in the process.

There have been repeated attempts, some successful, to back away from these policies and to return to an earlier era. The most important of these was the privatization of Conrail. This process, lasting from 1981 to 1987, once again effectively removed the federal government from the rail freight business, in spite of Conrail's profits from 1981 onward. This followed on the heels of the federal sale of the fully nationalized Alaska Railroad in 1981 to the State of Alaska, since no private-sector buyers were attracted. There have been repeated attempts to defund and to sell Amtrak, but these have been deflected by Congress. These attempts have resulted in slightly reduced appropriations for the line and drastically reduced morale for Amtrak personnel and certainly prevented needed rail passenger service expansion for the nation.

In assessing the contemporary era of rail public policy, we might say that it has been an incomplete departure from the culture of the U.S. political economy. The changes have been nondirect, incremental, and partial, as Herson theorized generally about public policy.[5] American public policy seldom changes radically and permanently within the space of a generation or less. The new era in rail public policy has not dealt substantially with many problem areas of the political economy of railroads. Taken as a whole, these untouched areas constitute an agenda for either a whole new public policy of railroading or a continuation of the present reform era, depending on how policy needs are characterized. The remaining public policy problems of railroading constitute issues for contemporary rail policymakers, if only by omission.

The most important aspect of these unresolved public rail

issues is the lack of governmental equity of treatment between modes of transportation. This needs to be evaluated by a judgment about the fairness of differences in governmental promotion of various modes of transportation,[6] for example, the different state and local property taxation policies caused by different federal provisions for transportation modes. The justice of relatively inequitable levels of modal subsidies needs to be examined, along with all other differences in federal transportation policy benefits for railroads and their competitors. Exactly equal federal treatment of transportation modes might not be just if situations differed radically between modes, but like treatments in like situations certainly are fair and should be part of a just public transportation policy. This has not been the case. The present promotions and subsidies of the various modes is patently inequitable.

Key terms are defined by Donald Harper as follows: "We define government *promotion* of transportation as any kind of financial or other government assistance to a carrier, including tax reduction programs, low cost or no cost and guaranteed loans, provision of facilities used by a carrier, the fall-out from government paid-for research and development programs that benefit carriers, and direct cash payments to carriers by government.... We define *subsidy* of transportation as existing whenever any part of a carrier's costs are borne by taxpayers and not by the carrier who benefits from government promotion."[7]

Historically, American government has not treated railroads as well as other transportation modes in like situations. In the present regulatory era, this situation has not ameliorated across the board, in spite of temporarily narrowed subsidy differentials due to heavy federal investment in Conrail through 1981 and continued investment in Amtrak. As Weaver puts it, "In the United States, federal rail spending began from a tiny base in 1970 [less than a tenth of a billion 1982 dollars]. Rapid spending growth in the 1970s was fueled primarily by the northeast rail crisis and federal support for Amtrak. Expenditures peaked in 1981 [at approximately $3.75 billion].... Federal rail expenditures in the United States declined substantially in the following years [totalling around $1.2 billion annually by 1985]. Subsidies to Amtrak compose the bulk of remaining outlays."[8]

It is useful to compare this to federal promotion and subsidy expenditures for other transportation modes in comparable years. Aggregate historical spending totals by mode are also illuminating in this context.

Harper uses Association of American Railroad figures when he writes: "Federal expenditures in the aggregate to assist transportation by air, highway, and water have increased over eleven times since 1952 ... to $10.7 billion in 1976."[9] These figures exclude all rail promotional spending, which totaled $2.1 billion in 1976 at the height of Conrail's formation and during the midst of the Amtrak modernization program, according to Weaver.[10]

Broken down by mode, the following figures from fiscal 1981 are illustrative. The year 1981 was chosen because it gives the most favorable comparison with other modes (most unfavorable to railroads) since American railroads received their all-time subsidy peak in federal expenditures in that year. Generally, other federal transportation spending has risen since that time, while rail spending has declined. In 1981, highways received about $9.5 billion in expenditures, with $341 million of that not covered by tax collections, user fees, and the $1.7 billion drawdown in 1981 of the Highway Trust Fund. Waterways and marine spending (excluding substantial U.S. Army Corps of Engineers outlays for waterways and marine transport) amounted to a $2.5 billion net subsidy, pipelines received $3 million, and air transportation received a net subsidy of $2.6 billion with $3.8 billion spent.[11] (Currently, it will be recalled, railroads receive around half-a-billion dollars net subsidy annually, excluding the money spent on Amtrak. In 1981, they received a $3.75 billion total.)

Looked at in a larger time frame, these figures take on additional meaning. The Board of Investigation and Research set up under the Transportation Act of 1940 calculated that railroads had received $627 million in total aid, including approximately $440 million in land grants designed to induce the post-Civil War building of the transcontinental railroads. It is generally agreed that the 50 percent tariff reduction to government transportation all railroads were mandated to give (repealed completely by 1945) amounted to a payback of more than the total figure. Given the value of dollars in those days, railroads, particularly western railroads, received great outlays in start-up funds in addition to the large annual federal rail expenditures of recent years.

In contrast, federal highway expenditures from 1921 to 1976 amounted to approximately $104 billion (with state and local expenditures adding $353 billion more). Current expenditures average around $6 billion per year. Airways have been recipients of large amounts of federal spending. They received about $20 billion between 1925 and 1976. Current annual expenditures run around $4 billion. Waterways, too, have received generous governmental promotion as a result of public policy — approximately $11.8 billion from the time of the early canals to 1976. Current net expenditures range well over $3 billion after the post-1978 user fees are subtracted and Corps of Engineers' related expenses are added. Urban mass passenger transportation system (highway and rail) have also received huge federal expenditures, but they are excluded from all of these figures because they are not analogous, being mostly local in impact.[12]

In retrospect, neither the total amounts of subsidies received by railroads for start-ups and rescues nor the distribution of those funds to a select few railroads rather than across the industry is comparable to what competing modes of transportation have received and continue to receive. This has been especially important in the 1980s as inequities have accelerated. Railroads have never regained their briefly held nineteenth century status of new industries deserving of public nurturing. At the same time, their not-so-new competitors have retained their favored place as beneficiaries of federal transportation development funds and policies designed to nurture new transportation industries. No tendencies for change in this inequity are evident in the immediate future. This has placed railroads at a major competitive disadvantage to other transport modes in the United States.

Another aspect of the equity question involves what transportation theorists refer to as "governmental provision of the ways." A great deal of federal promotion and subsidy of trucking, barge, and coastal water shipments, and airline operations involve government building and operating of roads, highways, waterways, airports, and airway navigation networks upon which these modes depend. While these subsidies are included in the aggregate net totals above, the totals do not reflect the fact that these subsidized ways are not owned by the modes in question. Therefore, they are not subject to state and local property taxes. Nor do the totals reflect the money the carriers with subsidized ways have available for other purposes, including that which winds up as profits. On the other hand, American railroads do not get their ways built and operated for them (not even Amtrak's Northeast Corridor was built by the government, although it was improved by public funds, as were some of Conrail's lines). As a result, U.S. railroads not only have to spend revenues for building and maintaining their rights of way (totalling $4.3 billion in 1985 for maintenance of way and structures alone), but also are obliged to pay state and local property taxes on their assessed values, amounting to an outlay of approximately $422 million in 1985.[13] This unfairness yields yet another inequity of railroad treatment vis-à-vis other modes.

Yet another aspect of the railroad equity issue involves the comparative modal externalities from the federal government's research and development programs. While the precise figures are speculative due to the secrecy of some of the data and the difficulty of assigning dollar figures to indirect payoffs, it is sensible to assume that the massive amounts of money spent by the U.S. armed services and the National Aeronautics and Space Administration on technological research and development benefit other modes of transportation more than they do railroads. This is because few dollars are spent on military or civilian rail research and development and many are spent on ships, airplanes, and wheeled land vehicles. Suffice it to say that the amount spent on the Federal Rail Transportation Test Center and other rail research and development is a minuscule fraction of what the Pentagon spends on land battlefield, naval, and aerospace research and development with application to civilian transportation technology.

Taken together, these facts and figures support the judgment that the U.S. government has not treated railroads as well as other transportation modes when each mode's importance in the national political economy is considered. This inequality apparently is not the result of conscious public policy. Instead, it stems from the federal desire to promote new modes of transportation coupled with the failure of policymakers to evaluate the long-term public-interest consequences of transportation policies. Each mode of transportation has historically received some promotional funds when young. Presumably, in the future, the "new" modes will receive fewer subsidies as they mature and as other, newer competing modes of transportation get federal attention and a share of available funds. Until that happens, however, railroads continue to be victimized by this public policy inequity. Rail competitors continue to be treated as new modes in spite of their states of development. They receive more than railroads do, their relative prosperity, social utility, and consequences for the national interest notwithstanding.

For purposes of argument, one may posit that all transportation modes are roughly equivalent in social utility. Consequently, to the extent that transportation subsidies are advisable public policies (an issue that will be touched upon in the following chapter), all modes ought to receive federal subsidies proportionately equal to their role in the national modal mix, with extra funds expended only for emergencies. Even without subsidy equity, the recent rail bankruptcy emergencies confronted by policymakers would have been less likely to happen if regulatory relief (partial deregulation) had come earlier than 1980, allowing the technological advantages of railroads to manifest themselves in a reasonably open transportation market. A sensible analytical approach looks beyond equity to assess how railroads are faring under contemporary federal transportation public policies and the state of rail economic regulatory policy in the post-Staggers Act era.

In the present less-regulated era, we find improvements over past eras. Relative equity in the weight and nature of economic regulation has been restored to competing modes, and each transportation mode has found an effective niche for its services. This has allowed the forces of the market to work as regulators, providing some justice while protecting the public interest through a safety net of regulatory protection for captive shippers. Railroad health has clearly improved, while the public interest has not suffered. Conclusive data to demonstrate this are not easily found, but it is significant to note that of the forty-five market dominance findings that have been made by the I.C.C. to date, shippers have won thirty-five, and six of the eight still pending on appeal have initial proshipper decisions.[14] This suggests that the "robber baron" has not returned in the era of partial rail deregulation policy. Clearly, the need for partial deregulation was real, and its consequences have allowed gains for all policy participants.

As impressive as the achievements of the rail regulatory reform movement have been,[15] problems of omission rather than commission remain in present public policies of transportation regulation. Important rail reform issues remain unresolved by Staggers and the other reform accomplishments, to the detriment of both railroads and the public interest. For example, still unclear is public policy on revenue adequacy of rail carriers. Standards for a fair rate of carrier return on investment exist but in practice remain largely symbolic, because profit shortfalls regularly occur and are not dealt with by policymakers. Instead, public policy continues to focus on legislated standards by setting maximum carrier rates. These are frequently irrelevant, because market conditions hold rates down below the maximums.[16] In the interim, rail carrier rates of return have actually dipped to below pre-Staggers levels.[17] The marketplace may take care of this in the future, but then again it may not. This is a problem policymakers must deal with if the long-term health of an industry dominated by privately held firms that depend on private sources for capital is to be maintained with any certainty.

Another area of rail regulatory policy ambiguity concerns federal policies of preserving competition and preventing monopolies through antitrust measures. Expressions of policy still on the books are designed to preserve competition intramodally and intermodally and to oppose mergers and acquisitions of other modes by all forms of transportation that are judged to be monopolistic or oligopolistic. However, the Staggers Act and other policies in place to maintain carrier revenue adequacy encourage some combinations and acquisitions. Again we see that expressions of national policy are inconsistent and policy implementation is ambiguous, often contradictory, and frequently more symbolic than real.

. Recently, some mergers (Burlington Northern, for one) and

some acquisitions (CSX acquiring Sea-Land, NS acquiring North American Van Lines) have been permitted, but the analogous Santa Fe-Southern Pacific combination has been denied. Congress, the Justice Department, the Transportation Department, and the I.C.C. frequently disagree on a single case. The ultimate resolution of these cases is by the courts or the market more often than not. (The Santa Fe-Southern Pacific merger was denied by the I.C.C. in 1987. Rather than endure lengthy and costly appeals, the railroads involved abandoned merger plans.)

Asch and Senaca suggest that "the basic question of what we mean by *competition* and *monopoly* have not been resolved by antitrust ... [and there is also] a need to define the market."[18] There are also problems and principled disagreements[19] with enforcement levels and impacts of policy that face potential merger and acquisition plans. The result is an area of policy ambiguity for the near future. This needs to be resolved in a definitive policy statute of the kind Lowi suggests,[20] so that railroads, other transportation markets, the investment community, and the federal government itself will have clear expectations about how the transportation environment of the twenty-first century will be shaped by public policies.

The social load — benefits for society in addition to ordinary business benefits — that public and private railroads are expected to carry in the future also needs to be clarified. How much social load, who is obligated to provide it, and who is expected to carry its costs need to be mandated. Clear and consistent public policy requires that public expectations of environmental protections for transportation providers, energy efficiency standards at both the carrier and the national level, and other social externalities be resolved and established for the future as well. They have not been under the present regulatory policy regime.

Transportation public policies need to clarify how mandated carrier goals are going to be implemented by the government in pursuit of the public interest. The choices are to rely on (1) partial economic regulation in an enhanced market political economy, (2) taxation and similar incentives to induce firm behavior, and (3) a combination of the two. With the passage of the Staggers Act and the Tax Reform Act of 1986, recent policy movement has been toward the first choice, though the others remain as options. U.S. legislative history suggests that this will change as these landmark statutes are "fine-tuned" by future policymakers facing different problems.

Given the policy ambiguities of the current rail policy era and the nondirect nature of U.S. public policy generally, what is the transportation public policy of the United States today? There is no comprehensive federal rail policy. Instead, a series of partial policies exists. Goals are general, and contradictory and/or symbolic implementation of these goals creates a partial vacuum that organized interests exploit.[21] The need for an overall rational and consistent national transportation policy has been recognized repeatedly in this century by policymakers in their attempts to convene study commissions on the subject. None of the commissions has resulted in effective, comprehensive policy setting legislation and implementation. The most recent attempt was the National Transportation Policy Study Commission convened in 1976, which turned in its voluminous final report to President Carter in June 1979. Its indirect justification of deregulation added fuel to the regulatory reform movement, but its many other policy recommendations and predictions for a sound and rational national transportation policy were effectively shelved by the Reagan administration. This practice has been the rule rather than the exception since the Wilson administration.[22]

The implications of a lack of policy are straightforward. First of all, federal rail policy is active and vigorous only in times of crisis or transition in the rail political economy. The quasi-nationalizations of the National Railroad Passenger Corporation and the Consolidated Rail Corporation as reactions to crises of service and the privatization of Consolidated Rail that took place as a result of the pro-laissez-faire policy momentum generated by the 1980 national elections illustrate this point. In normal times, de facto federal rail policy is to wait for such crises or major problems to emerge and then to deal with them hurriedly and incrementally. The occasional successes of the de facto policies do not negate the essential point that recent rail public policy is characterized by neglect — it is *non*-policy. Normal times in the U.S. rail political economy are devoid of long-range planning or "rail intelligence," and largely uncoordinated with the efforts of states and local governments to regulate and otherwise deal with rail transportation. Thus, events are not anticipated, and solutions to emerging problems are not carefully evaluated before they must be implemented swiftly in the face of mounting public pressure. No principles or policies of ownership and operation of rail transportation based upon a sound application of the political theory of public utilities have emerged or are likely to do so under this policy environment.

In freight transportation the tendency to move away from rail planning and intelligence has manifested itself most strongly in the failure to develop an integrated transportation systems policy. Railroads, trucking firms, airlines, barge operators, and pipe-line operators all operate in a competitive transportation market and generally rely on their own resources for the sale of their transportation services. It is up to them to decide what routes and equipment are best, and frequently the markets and existing resources dictate choices without regard to social externalities or long-range corporate needs. The economies of scale and diversification that characterize integrated national transportation firms like the Canadian Pacific and the Canadian National are absent in the United States, because public policy has not clearly mandated them in the present and has forbidden them in the past at times. Consequently, Canadian transport firms enjoy advantages denied their American counterparts. Currently, U.S. transcontinental rail shipments must travel on more than one railroad line, increasing costs, paperwork, and the opportunities for delay. No transcontinental railroads exist because of public policy and carrier inertia caused by past experiences. Intermodalism as a public policy similarly suffers, since it is not clear how much intermodal cooperation, coordination, and ownership is approved by policymakers and how much is not. Intermodal shipments do exist, but their technological ability to dominate the transportation market to the benefit of railroads is deterred, at least partially, by the failure of policymakers to create clear enabling legislation and/or economic incentives for them.

In rail passenger transportation, similar nonpolicy manifestations abound. Intercity carriage is by means of the quasi-nationalized Amtrak, which operates skeletal, infrequent service outside of the Boston-Washington corridor in competition with airlines, buses, and automobiles. The appropriate role of passenger trains as frequent, high-speed corridor haulers for most short and intermediate trips has not been realized or developed by policymakers. Also, statelization and localization abounds for commuter and urban passenger haulage, which is also in competition with other modes. No clear national policy of efficient modal use, of the appropriate mix of ownership of firms, or of fulfilling the long-range passenger transportation needs of the nation exists. In its stead, there is continued highway and airway promotion and a year-by-year look at the deficits of rail passenger transportation coupled with an occasional cry by government "planners" to sell off Amtrak[23] or to go on funding its present range of services for another fiscal period.

The most significant manifestations of this climate of rail public policy in the United States is the avoidance by policymakers of their responsibility to allocate national transportation needs in the public interest. In other words, policies currently rely on the mechanism of government-enhanced free markets to allocate transportation needs, and efficiency and national needs suffer.

In his seminal study of analogous processes, McConnell says that appropriate prescriptions for the national interest "include reassertion of public values and a clear understanding of the means by which these may be achieved.... They require rejection of the illusion that informality of government produces justice, that political power can be abolished, and that the surrender of public authority to private hands results in democracy. None of these requirements are radical."[24]

In the same vein, Walsh argues that the many public corporations in the American political economy have emerged because public authorities find them convenient vehicles through which to evade both the inefficient allocative powers of the market and electoral mandates. Though these public entities are by definition political in their operations, they do not allocate services well, because they, too, respond to sectarian concerns due to their limited scope.[25] If the public interest is to be served, transportation allocation must be regulated at the national level, taking the interests of both public and private carriers, shippers, travelers, and the nation into account. That can be accomplished only by a national democratic process that forces national public policymakers to respond to national planners and full public debate.

No assessment of the current rail public policies in the United States is complete without an examination of the institutional complex that public policies filter through as they are implemented. Keep in mind the earlier analysis of the extremely complicated structure of the government of the United States, which combines federalism and separation of powers and allocates public policy through approximately 86,000 governments. Our assessment will zoom in on the institutional matrix of one government in that system, the national government of the United States. It displays a Byzantine complexity of transportation policy-allocating institutions that complicates transportation policy-making and implementation.

On the congressional level, the Senate Commerce Committee and Public Works Committee and the House committees on Interstate and Foreign Commerce, Public Works and Transportation, and Merchant Marine and Fisheries (together with the numerous subcommittees of each major committee) hold primary rail and rail-impacting transportation policy jurisdiction. In most cases, these committees effectively control the flow of transportation-related bills. However, they share policy-making authority with other congressional committees such as House Appropriations, House Government Operations, Senate Judiciary, House Post Office and Civil Service, House Ways and Means, Senate Finance, House Education and Labor, and Senate Labor and Public Welfare[26] and their many subcommittees. Also frequently playing a policy role, as conditions warrant, are joint conference committees and special investigatory committees.

In order to make effective policy, any public-policy-making body depends upon its understanding of the problems and its ability to evaluate potential solutions. Consequently, all of these transportation policy-setting bodies are heavily dependent upon the fact-finding and analytical abilities of their own staffs and members as well as the information and intelligence gathering facilities of the General Accounting Office, the Legislative Reference Service of the Library of Congress, and the Congressional Budget Office. Accordingly, each of these support structures must also be considered part of the congressional transportation institutional complex.

The executive branch institutional complex dealing either directly or indirectly with rail transportation is no less complicated than the legislative branch complex. Transportation policy-making is shared by the White House (president, vice president, advisors, and staff, including the Office of Management and Budget, the Council of Economic Advisors, and so on) and the massive Department of Transportation. The D.O.T. includes the National Transportation Safety Board, Coast Guard, Federal Aviation Administration, National Highway Transportation Safety Administration, Federal Highway Administration, Federal Railroad Administration (no trucking administration exists), St. Lawrence Seaway Development Corporation, Urban Mass Transit Administration, and Material Transportation Bureau, along with many departments and subagencies belonging to each major "administration."[27]

Other cabinet-level agencies, like the Department of Commerce, Department of Justice, and Department of Labor, also share important and regular transportation policy roles with D.O.T. But virtually every executive agency or department from State to Defense has some transportation policy interest and authority, and all of them touch rail transportation occasionally if not continually. For example, even the U.S. Air Force owns a tiny fleet of locomotives for use at bases and is investigating the possibility of basing mobile intercontinental ballistic missiles on trains, as is the current practice in the U.S.S.R. Nuclear warheads are also regularly transported by train in the continental United States. Such practices create interest in the rail system. And where interest lies in the government, the desire to make policy lurks nearby.

Also sharing executive transportation policy-making are the various federal independent regulatory commissions. Currently, these include the Federal Maritime Commission and the Interstate Commerce Commission, since the Civil Aeronautics Board was abolished in the recent regulatory reform movement. While theoretically independent, these commissions respond to executive pressure through the appointment and legislation-recommending processes. The I.C.C. is still an important transportation public policy maker in the aftermath of partial deregulation. It currently plays an important role in administering the Staggers Act and in setting precedents for future rail mergers and intermodal affairs as well as regulating the trucking industry.

The judicial branch of the federal government is involved in transportation policy setting. The courts play a major role in American business policy adjudication, and it is difficult to draw a clear distinction between judicial practices interpreting the law and judicial policy-making. It is reasonable to suggest that both go on regularly, particularly in the absence of a clear, united policy-making voice from the other branches of government. Appeals on the decisions of the independent regulatory commissions go first to the federal courts of appeal (bypassing the pre-1975 jurisdiction of federal district courts) and then to the Supreme Court.[28] The courts hear appeals on settlement of the estates of bankrupt rail firms, are the final adjudicators of rail labor cases, and can set the tone on mergers, consolidations, antitrust issues, regulatory scope, and a wide spectrum of rail-relevant issues.

Finally, the National Railroad Passenger Corporation is also a federal transportation entity, as was Conrail before 1987. Its active intragovernmental lobbying and its quasi-public relationship to other railroads and state and local jurisdictions give it a share of federal rail policy.

Clearly, federal rail policy is made through a complex institutional matrix that affects it and those who deal with it. Not only are there many agencies and authorities with potential policy-making authority (whether direct or indirect, major or minor), but these agencies are not fixed in their relationships to one another or to their constituents. Agency policy-setting roles shift with changes in topics on the effective policy agenda, the personalities involved, perceptions of the latest electoral results, and the effectiveness of interests in articulating their points of view. They also change as a given policy moves along the various phases of the policy process from initiation to termination.[29] An issue as persistent over time and as critical to the national interest as rail transportation pervades each important nook and cranny of the most complex government in the world at one time or another.

The implications of this complexity and pervasiveness are obvious. The task of state and local transportation policy agencies and the individual transportation firms in influencing policy that affects them is made very difficult by having to deal with this immense bureaucracy. Since the system is so difficult to move in a coordinated fashion, changes become unlikely except in emergencies. The result is policy inertia, policy contradiction, and policy inefficiency in process and practice. Failure to clearly define federal policy goals and attempts to implement ambiguous policy agendas through a difficult-to-negotiate maze of structural complexity and overlapping jursidiction leads to a de facto nonpolicy of federal transportation policy-making except in times of crisis. As Lowi has suggested, it leads to a government that cannot plan effectively.[30]

Past as Prologue:
Rail Policy Agenda of the Near Future

Regardless of the nondirect and status quo biases of policy-making in the United States, changes do happen. Policymakers respond to events and needs, however imperfect the process might be, in either an absolute or a comparative sense and however much these responses seem to come in waves. However, such waves of change cannot be counted upon as long-term reform vehicles, since they dissipate rapidly. Accordingly, it makes sense to assume that the recent wave in rail policy-making has essentially played itself out with the privatization of Conrail, the stabilization of Amtrak as a limited, subsidized system, and the regularization of Staggers Act enforcement. These have become the status quo and have acquired significant constituencies to fight for them. They are likely to persist in the near future because of the status quo biases of the system and the apparent lack of rail crises that could be catalysts for a new wave of rail public policy activism.

Given that the political economy of rail transportation in America has not been permanently altered by responses to the crises of the last generation, it is a useful exercise in policy analysis to project the near future of rail policy on the basis of an essentially unchanged present. Projecting the future is always a risky business, but risks can be minimized if projections are not extended too far out in time and if they are based upon present trends. The culture of the American political economy and public policy analysis are useful guides to the process.

The first projection that should be made is that there is not likely to be any consistent and effective long-range planning for rail public policy in the future, because nothing has been done to bring it about. Thus, the next crises are likely to hit without warning and preparation, putting key policymakers at a disadvantage once again. This is not to say that no transportation planning takes place at the federal level in the United States. According to Sampson, Farris, and Shrock, "the last two or three decades have seen an era of transportation planning ... in (1) transportation system development...; (2) transportation administration and planning...; (3) passenger transportation development...; (4) regional railroad transportation planning...; and (5) environmental and energy concerns.... In each of these areas, the programs involved generally have been characterized by direct congressional action, crash programs to solve pressing problems, avoidance of nationalization, and massive amounts of federal aid, with local participation whenever possible."[31]

As Lowi's analysis of the original I.C.C. statute and implementation demonstrates, it was successful government planning only because it contained "a fairly clear specification of standards regarding jurisdiction of the Commission and regarding the behavior of the railroad deemed unlawful ... [and] the Act itself was the culmination of a long history of public efforts vis-à-vis rail service and rates, efforts in State Law and in the common law. In effect, congressional language, even where vague, had been 'freighted with meaning' by history."[32]

These perspectives demonstrate that government public planning is possible in rail areas. However, Lowi's point is that it is rare and requires special conditions. He makes the further point that such conditions are usually not present in governments that have structures similar to that of the United States. Sampson, Farris, and Shrock's observations also suggest that what transportation planning does take place is severely limited in scope and time. It addresses specific questions while ignoring overall policy linkages and is designed as a reaction or a "quick fix" for the short run. Conrail and Amtrak certainly fall in this category.

The privatization of Conrail and the pursuit of regulatory reform that relies heavily on the market for regulation also demonstrate that the political culture that Herson, Hartz, Dolbeare, Phelps, and others have stressed in their analyses continues to play a large role in U.S. rail transportation policy. Reliance on the market is virtually a reflex action in policy-making. In fact, it is so common that policies that deviate from the market norm commonly are reversed or vitiated if opportunities to do so exist. This of course was the case with Conrail, made valuable to the private sector by public improvement, and is not the case with Amtrak, because its operating results are not attractive to the private sector.

These tendencies are not necessarily bad, of course. Staggers and the limited use of quasi-nationalization succeeded where previous policies had not (the jury is still out on Conrail's privatization). When they become virtually automatic and are policy goals to be pursued regardless of their appropriateness to a given situation, they may become counter productive. When future rail crises hit, it is unclear whether such policy tendencies will serve the public interest. The historical record of rail policy-making in the United States is a mix of successes and failures.

Since present policies are not causing imminent crisis, we may predict on the basis of U.S. rail policy precedents that the present interest in monitoring the effectiveness of rail policies and planning for the next crisis will dissipate without results. The immediate future is unlikely to see any changes brought about by wholesale public policy planning. No matter what near future electoral results will bring, there is little likelihood of any future nationalizations or quasi-nationalizations of rail properties (barring a radical change in the effects of present policies brought about by a national emergency).

Other characteristics of U.S. rail policy for the near future are less predictable. Still, plausible scenarios emerge as a function of projecting the present without systematic change. Most important of these is that the inequities of modal treatment regarding subsidy and provision of ways is not likely to be altered in any important way. Rail subsidies are tapering off, and recent legislation reacting to air traffic safety crises and the desire to complete and repair the interstate highway system will likely result in ever-higher levels of subsidies for those modes.[33]

The highway model of way development, ownership, and operation is a precedent for U.S. transportation policy that is not likely to spread to rails, in spite of the urgings of a spectrum of prominent transportation journalists like Kneiling and Phillips.[34] It is unlikely that the federal government will purchase or otherwise acquire railroad main and branch lines (or even terminal facilities) from their present owners and bring them up to high standards of operation where necessary, install nationally consistent state-of-the-art communications and signal devices and then open them to all comers who can meet license standards of safety and interchangeability of equipment, and require the payment of user fees. Such a scenario is likely to be too costly and meet too much opposition by present rail owners and operators to be seriously considered, in spite of its equity and other externality payoffs.

Another likely scenario in the near future of U.S. rail policy is the continued purposeful avoidance of a proactive public policy of public and private competition of rail systems on the Canadian model (rather than private system competing with private system). The U.S. government's ownership of the quasi-nationalized Conrail almost brought about that policy by default. Conrail's marketplace competition with Norfolk Southern and CSX was vigorous and surely resulted in operating efficiencies for all concerned. In effect, the federal policy became an inadvertent one of regulation through demonstration in the rail political economy via the Consolidated Rail Corporation, in the manner of the Tennessee Valley Authority and the corporations analyzed by Musolf and Walsh.[35] Privatization ended that policy-by-default, and its resumption is unlikely because of the power of the political culture, vested interests, and budgetary considerations. Amtrak, of course, does not serve that function, since it has no real rail competition, and it is not yet a model of efficiency or cost-effectiveness, even though it does take some revenues away from airlines and bus operators.

Uncle Sam's quasi-nationalized passenger railroad is likely to continue in its present form and scope for the foreseeable future, for it is not a saleable property and the need for passenger train service remains. Barring a long, production-centered war that siphons off highway travel resources, as did World War II, or an oil crisis that is more sustained and serious than past crises, Amtrak is unlikely to receive the massive infusion of resources and line expansions that would allow the system to "take off" in the manner of European rail passenger transportation systems after World War II. In the absence of national planning and policy priorities that take externalities (benefits and costs extrinsic to the enterprise, such as environmental concerns) into account, the costs of electrification, widespread and frequent high-speed corridor service, and renewal of freight lines to passenger service standards are simply prohibitive. Thus, those improvements will not be propelled onto the national rail policy priority agenda by ordinary airway and highway passenger overutilization and its resulting inconvenience or by recognition of the overall social utility of rail passenger transportation. Consequently, rail subsidies of needed services are likely to continue to be borne by sub-federal governments under section 403(b) of the Rail Passenger Service Act in an inconsistent and underutilized manner and as state and local planning processes dictate and resources permit. Ambitious plans by the states of Florida, California, Pennsylvania, Ohio, and others to build or contract to private enterprise their own high-speed rail passenger networks (with the eventual possibility of the lines being taken over by an Amtrak-like federal operation) are not likely to materialize in any important manner without federal aid. Such aid will not be forthcoming in the near future.

Consistent with this, another relatively simple prediction to make is that the general integration of externalities into the future development and use of the national railroad system is unlikely, given the absence of both effective national rail planning and effective continuing national transportation planning generally. Thus, it makes sense to assume that the advantages of the flanged steel wheel rolling on steel rail will not be fully utilized in the near future U.S. political economy. And the freight and passenger modal mix will continue to be inefficient and accidental. This is unfortunate because railroads hold enormous potential for economic development assistance, energy efficiency, urban planning, efficient land use, and foreign energy-source independence in the future political economy. Even as the often-predicted partial transition to a service economy and away from an industrial economy takes place, potential railroad externalities are unlikely to diminish substantially. The United States, a nation of 250 million literate people with an industrial tradition and infrastructure, will continue to have an important industrial base that will need railroads for freight transportation and for passenger service, if only to combat gridlock. Even the service economy will find many externalities associated with railroads, as has been the case in Japanese and French business and pleasure utilization of rail passenger service.

The conclusion seems irresistible: given the prediction of lack of substantial rail public policy changes in the United States in the near future, a major expansion or contraction of the level of rail service as a result of public policy is improbable. Any changes in level of rail service that come will originate in the private sector as it continues to react to the public rail policy environment and the profit motive. Since government-enhanced markets only imperfectly take externalities into account, the changes that arise in that way are not likely to be externality propelled or take the needs of the nation into account effectively. Nor are they likely to be of sufficient magnitude to cure the nation's rail policy ills.

The largely unplanned transportation market of the near future might result in the continued expansion of economically attractive intermodal container service (in import, export, transcontinental land-bridge, and domestic service) and the continued slow growth of rail demand. However, it could just as plausibly result in the leveling off of such services and demand. That, in turn, would signal a return to the long-term tendency in this century of gradual decline of rail service as a share of total intercity freight transportation as the advantages of the regulatory reform movement are fully utilized, since no new regulatory reform initiatives are foreseen. Prediction in this area depends upon the fate of industrialization in the United States, so is tricky to formulate.

A less tentative prediction can be made in the area of public policy dealings with future rail redundancies, bankruptcies, and emerging short lines and regional railroads. Here, too, the lack of effective national rail transportation planning and the de facto nonpolicy of public rail policy will take their toll. The post-Conrail bankruptcies of the Chicago, Rock Island, and Pacific and the Chicago, Milwaukee, St. Paul and Pacific railroads did not result in quasi-nationalizations or new policy initiatives. By the time they reached the policy front-burner, the federal government was short of funds and exhausted by dealing with rail policy.[36] The federal policy response was typically nondirect, giving yet another signal that the old regime is not dead.

The emergence of about one hundred eighty shortlines and regional railroads since 1980[37] also has not resulted in federal policy initiatives. Here, too, the nondirect nature of public policy rules. It is unlikely that acceleration of these trends (caused by railroad attempts to become more efficient as revenues dwindle) will be a catalyst for important rail policy changes. The several hundred regional and short-line railroads in existence will have to make it on their own under the present policy regime. A national policy of either incentives for private enterprise or quasi-nationalization on the highway model would be appropriate to prevent these new properties from going bankrupt or cutting back on service. Jobs would be preserved and these feeder lines would bring business to Class I railroads. One of these policies (or one that allows integrated national transportation firms to plan to acquire light-density lines with the security of long-term policy protection and incentives) would be in the national interest. But rail public policy will probably ignore this issue unless a crisis looms.

Conclusion

Rail public policy in the near future will resemble the rail public policy of the present. No crises of sufficient magnitude to propel rail policy change to the front of the public policy agenda are imminent and probably will not occur for the remainder of this century. The inconveniences and inefficiencies of present policies will be tolerated in spite of occasional grumblings by academics or affected interests.

Nevertheless, the rail problems of the near future constitute an agenda for public rail policy for the remainder of this century. A rational, integrated, planned public policy of rail transportation is needed. Policymakers have an opportunity to seize on their inconveniences and costs and create an American Bahn 2000, even though the way will not be easy. Bahn 2000 has been described as "an ambitious project of the Swiss Federal Railways ... for a complete reorganization of the schedule system and infrastructure of the Swiss Federal Railways and the privately owned railroads as well as the postal bus system.... [It is] a carefully thought out plan of coordination which takes into account the size of the country and its particular geographic structure.... [It will] create a rail system by the end of the century that can compete successfully with the private automobile. Werner Latscha, the president for the general management of the Swiss Federal System called 'Bahn 2000' the 'last real possibility to create a transportation system that is socially and ecologically sound.'"[38] However, such a plan is not likely to be incorporated into American policy.

It is worth stressing again that current nondirect rail public policy is not working well in the rail political economy of the United States, though it is an improvement over what preceded it. Major modifications of public rail policy will not come unless a crisis of sufficient magnitude to make another reform era in American rail public policy irresistible is perceived by the policy community, or unless policymakers use all the political skills at their disposal to convince the nation that something better can be brought about. In spite of the need for institutional streamlining in public rail transportation policy-making and better transportation planning, in spite of the disadvantages for the public interest of allowing private allocation of public needs, and in spite of the need to replace accidental and crisis-driven policy implementation with an effective long-range rail policy, like a stalled freight train on a grade, only a powerful force can put these in motion. The final chapter prescribes some needed changes and briefly assesses their significance and political and philosophical utility for the political economy of railroading in the not-so-immediate future.

chapter five

Rail Public Policy: Perspectives and Prescriptions

FROM THEIR ORIGINS TO THE PRESENT, railroads have affected many areas of interest to governments. Today, railroads remain both a barometer of and a catalyst for change in modern, industrialized political economies. Though trains and tracks may be overshadowed in the headlines and on policy agendas by strategic arms policies, international trade, and industrial competitiveness, their technology remains indispensable. They continue to have the potential to positively affect national land and energy usage and the quality of the physical environment. They can also affect industrial efficiency and competitiveness and the general quality of life in the United States. Consequently, they continue to be an appropriate focal point of public policy more than a century and a half after the first steam locomotive chugged along an iron-strapped wooden track.

What should the public policy of the United States be toward rail transportation? Herson's philosophical perspective led him to conclude that "perhaps the ultimate paradox of an inquiry into American public policy is contained in the idea that continuity is to be maintained only by admitting change. In that idea we find the essence of American political thought and the politics of ideas that drives it."[1]

Nagel's approach as a policy scientist led him to observe that "policy evaluation is more likely to be used [by public policy makers] when: (1) it is communicated well, (2) there is low opposition and possibly high support, (3) the communication is to the appropriate government decision makers, (4) it relates to the intended goals of the decision makers, and (5) it produces more benefits than costs in the eyes of the decision makers."[2]

Stiglitz's point of view was undoubtedly informed by his role as a public sector economist. He wrote, "When economists make [normative] statements, they try not to impose ... their own values. They often view themselves as providing 'technical assistance' to policymakers, ... and when they are in conflict, to suggest how these conflicts can be resolved.... Economists' work on these questions often comes close to that of political philosophers."[3]

Taking these perspectives and data presented in preceding chapters together, we are led to conclude that the politics of industrial change is not a random occurrence — it can be managed. What is more, sound public policy planning and analysis show that the future of the nation will be well served by more rational rail policies. Such public management of a major transportation resource will help the nation transform the inevitable industrial changes of the near future from problems to opportunities.

The changes necessitated by such management can be accomplished by policymakers if some of the conditions that Nagel describes are present or can be created.[4] If Herson is correct, change cannot be avoided. Our only option is to manage it. But what kind of change ought to take place and who will manage it toward what end? The answers are partly empirical and partly normative. Ultimately, prescription is a valid goal (some would say an obligation) of those who labor in policy analysis and who want to improve the world they live in, as Stiglitz and others not normally associated with normative political theory recognize. Even the smallest changes will not come easily, given the nondirect nature of U.S. policy.

As we ask what ought to be done about public policy toward railroad transportation in the United States, we should recognize that American-style rail policies are neither divinely ordained nor inevitable historical forces. They are simply the legacies of past cultural, political, and economic choices made by people attempting to cope with crises, self-interest, perceptions of the public interest, ideology, values, and so on. What has been shaped can be reshaped if people see the need for different policies, and they have the knowledge to know what to do to bring them about.

Perspectives and Lessons

Among the many lessons we should draw from analysis of rail public policy one of the most fundamental concerns the boundaries of practical change in the American political economy. Of the many models of rail political economy, two illustrate the parameters of acceptable change in transportation organization in a system of nondirect policy. Any change that goes beyond the parameters is likely to run into opposition; the "un-American" nature of the projected change will become the issue rather than any merits it may contain.

One of the two models is the government-enhanced market model that evolved from the Jacksonian period to the present. The other is the Canadian or quasi-nationalized model characterized by quasi-public and private rail enterprises in competition with each other. Either is adaptable to the American rail political economy of the present and future.

Under the U.S. model (ignoring the role of Amtrak, which has no effective railroad competition for the passenger hauling market), public policies and traditions have produced a market designed to foster competition between many regional, privately owned rail common carriers. In most cases, when private alternatives exist, policymakers see the role of government as being an overseer rather than a direct participator. The government's legitimate policy functions are to regulate safety and environmental impacts of rail activities and the nature and level of competition. Economic decisions by carriers are regulated by market forces except in cases of "market dominance." It is assumed that the market serves the consumer and carrier alike while it allocates appropriate levels of freight rail transportation for the nation. In effect, the government serves as a "night watchman," protecting the system from unwarranted interference and allowing the managers of the enterprise to run things.

As we have seen, such assumptions are only partially warranted. In spite of the existence of unresolved problems, current U.S. rail freight transportation is profitable in the aggregate, thus serving the needs of carriers. Shippers are served because the I.C.C. experience with rate challenges demonstrates that consumers (rail shippers) are treated fairly if they take advantage of the due process afforded them. Also, the system does a fair job in allocating freight transportation because most areas of the nation have some level of rail service, albeit less than many desire.

The Canadian model, on the other hand, encompasses a more active role for government and public policy in the national rail political economy.[5] Under this form of rail organization, the government directly owns and indirectly operates (through quasi-nationalization) the Canadian National system (CN), a rail-based integrated transportation provider serving the whole nation. The CN serves as the competition for the other major freight hauler in Canada, the Canadian Pacific (CP), a similar rail-based integrated transportation provider. The free market for rail and other freight transportation by common carrier still exists, but it is more limited in Canada than in the United States in that it consists of only two main competitors. (VIA, an Amtrak-like quasi-nationalized rail passenger system, is not considered in our analysis, just as we are not including Amtrak. Also, freight short lines exist in Canada, but to a much lesser extent than they do in the United States.) The competition (quite vigorous in places) within the market is between a public and a private entity.

The Canadian government is enhancing the market for rail transportation in Canada by direct participation through a "commercial Crown corporation." It has done so since 1919, when Ottawa rescued failing transcontinental rail lines in a Conrail-style takeover to form the CN.[6] The government railroad plays by the same rules and has the same social-service expectations (and subsidies for them, where necessary) as its private competitor. As a result, the market conditions for genuine competition between CN and CP are ensured.

Competition between public and private rail sectors is intense, perhaps more intense than it is between private systems. This resembles the situation in the United States when Conrail began to successfully compete with other regional American railroads in the profitable years preceding privatization. Rail service in Canada to remote areas is also somewhat denser than in the United States (although the government currently has a policy of trimming that back), and financial results are comparable. When subsidized social-service mandates are removed from the equation, "Canada's railways are the most productive in the world by most statistical measures, despite the operating problems posed by terrain and climate."[7]

It is assumed that this kind of competition is healthy for railroads and their customers. Such an assumption is warranted by the performance of the Canadian rail freight system. Carriers, the public, and shippers are all relatively well served, although the deficits incurred for social services are a matter of national debate. Though post-Trudeau governments have been committed to trimming the costs of running the rail system, direct government presence within the rail political economy has become a part of the Canadian political culture. It remains a long-standing Canadian public policy that any market defects in allocating rail transportation will be rectified in the public interest by a combination of universal social-service mandates and direct, subsidized rail service by the Canadian National acting as a government provider.

Thus, the two models can be assumed to be the effective parameters of "saleable" rail policy changes in the U.S. rail political economy. Either one could work in either system. In fact, elements of the Canadian model were present in the quasi-nationalized Conrail period of 1976 to 1987 in the United States. Culturally, the U.S. political economy will embrace either model, even though there is a smaller constituency for nationalization in the United States than there is in Canada. Because quasi-nationalization as a political economy relies heavily on an enhanced market and can be shown to be quite different than the European and Japanese direct nationalization of railroads, American political culture would accept it, albeit with opposition from the right wing of American politics. Because of the precedent of success set by Conrail, we conclude that elements of the Canadian model are exportable to the rail political economy of the United States if conditions warrant. However, the possibility of a reversal of policy and a reprivatization of future quasi-nationalizations is always present.

Socialism and the pure market, or regulation only by the market place, are not practical policies in the United States for railroads or any other sector of the economy. Pure socialism (or anything perceived to be closely related to it) has not taken root in the United States because of the dominance of the liberal traditions, both classical and social reform, and it will remain the target of fierce opposition. A pure market economy still has some ideological adherents, but the industrial and postindustrial experiences of the United States long ago led policymakers of the nation to abandon it and to gain public acceptance for their programs if not their ideology. Consequently, the U.S. political culture has occupied a middle ground. It has embraced a tradition and practice of mixed political economy with significant amounts of government intervention into many areas, including railroads.

While memories of recent rail crises and government interventions are still fresh, it should not be difficult to convince all but the most ultraconservative policymakers that the federal government should have an important role to play in setting railroad policy. Washington must be more than a night watchman empowered by the I.C.C.'s "captive shipper" protections mandated by Staggers, and Amtrak should continue to operate. The recent privatization of Conrail came at the crest of a wave of laissez-faire policy, and a future crisis of rail freight service might bring about a wave of re-quasi-nationalization as powerful as that of privatization.

Another lesson to be drawn from this is that the present nondirect policies have allowed opportunities to be lost for a nation struggling for industrial competitiveness. Although the rail infrastructure of the nation is not in crisis now, the catalogue of rail policy problems cannot be ignored. Present public policies have not allocated rail transportation services in the best interests of the nation. The solution of the northeast rail crisis, a partial solution to the rail passenger crisis, and a small boost to private railroads in the United States have benefitted the nation. But they have not prevented costly transportation subsidy inequity, underutilization of railroads, overutilization of less efficient transportation modes, and inefficiencies of present policy-making structures. And they have prevented economies of scale and other efficiencies by blocking integrated national transportation firms.

Another important lesson is drawn from an assessment of recent national experiences with Conrail and Amtrak. Given the parameters of the American culture, quasi-nationalization was the only viable option for policymakers facing the bankruptcy of the Penn-Central and other regional railroads. As Musolf[8] has demonstrated, full nationalization would have met a firestorm of opposition, and private-sector solutions would have failed quickly. Quasi-nationalization worked even though it became public policy by default. The financial turnaround of the Consolidated Rail Corporation could not have been accomplished without the deep pockets of the federal government. And, the successful attraction of investors for privatization of Conrail would not have been possible without a policy of quasi-nationalization.

Comparison of Conrail with the National Railroad Passenger Corporation reinforces this lesson. Amtrak's limited service and financial turnaround was accomplished by default; the quasi-nationalization of Conrail was emulated gradually as other options were discredited. While the prospects of a Conrail-like resurgence of Amtrak are dim, due to the nature of rail passenger service conditions, quasi-nationalization has worked here, too. The lesson is clear: quasi-nationalizations of rail properties in the United States work and can be enacted in the face of crisis or of conditions approximating those described by Nagel.

The success to date of a private Conrail (often cited by critics of direct government participation in the rail political economy to show the bankruptcy of that policy) is beside the point. A continuation of government direction of Conrail surely would have brought continued operating and service successes, without giving up the benefits of regulation-by-doing that characterized Conrail's presence in the political economy.

The last major lesson to be drawn from recent U.S. rail experiences is that detailed economic regulation of railroads does not work well within the American political economy. Too often, regulations are policymakers' hurried reactions to the political pressures borne of crisis and therefore are not planned thoroughly. Even when they are well-conceived, they are prone to quick obsolescence by changing conditions in the political economy. Consequently, the long-term inefficiencies of such regulations are not evaluated and taken into account. "The multiple veto points within the federal government"[9] and the extremely complex structure of U.S. policy-making make it difficult to change policies even if they are perceived to be faulty. Hence, detailed economic regulation becomes inefficient for carriers or shippers with the passage of time, irrespective of its original wisdom. Clearly, other regulatory alternatives are preferable.

The goals of the rail regulatory reform movement of the 1970s and 1980s were laudable. Partial deregulation has worked because it has been backed up by economic regulations via I.C.C. investigations of market dominance cases and by vigorous and detailed enforcement of safety and environmental regulations. In order for these policies to remain successful, however, they must be monitored continually and changed only to the extent that they remain effective in changing conditions. Any needed alterations must be formulated with accurate projection of costs, benefits, and external consequences. They must also be monitored through an institutional complex that is more responsive to the public interest and less responsive to particular affected interests than is presently the case.

Prescriptions: A Minimalist Approach

Lessons should lead to conclusions and conclusions to prescriptions for policy changes. While errors will be made as new policies are enacted and events are not correctly anticipated, avoiding repetition of past errors would be no small achievement. Accordingly, the prescriptions that follow take the lessons into account. In large measure, the prescriptions are formulated by the lessons, just as patriotism or revolution results from an assessment of the values a political system upholds and how well the system performs.[10]

The most important thing policymakers can do to accomplish a better rail policy is to determine and then execute the proper overall role of government and public policy in the U.S. political economy of transportation. Western political theory of public utilities asserts that good transportation is a basic necessity for a nation. It also suggests that government ought either to directly provide transportation or to oversee its indirect allocation as part of a government's obligation to provide a basic infrastructure of utilities for the public interest.

Taking into account the traditions, budget needs, and other priorities of the U.S. government, policymakers ought to take a more direct role in allocating transportation delivery systems. Since the market has proven to be a good allocator of transportation once it is enhanced by appropriate government action, Congress ought to enact a statute specifying that the government regulate transportation just enough to make certain that the market works and no more. That statute would commit the federal government directly or indirectly to provide all localities with adequate common-carrier freight and passenger service. It ought to further specify that redundant (hence inefficient) services not be subsidized or otherwise supported by public policy. Also, it should be a matter of law that inappropriate use of transportation modes are not protected by government, for example, short-haul air service that can be better accomplished by high-speed corridor rail passenger service; light-density rail freight routes that can be served best by short-haul trucks carrying intermodal containers to the nearest main rail line; long-haul trucking between major points that can be served best by intermodal rail service combined with short-haul road pick up and delivery, and so on.

Undesirable services do not need to be outlawed. They should simply be denied subsidies of any kind, because they are contrary to the national interest. The money saved in not paying unnecessary subsidies (and the money gained from profits from future quasi-nationalizations and transportation user fees) should be earmarked to pay for needed improvements and to establish a permanent, effective transportation planning presence in the U.S. government.

As part of general policy, it ought to be made clear which transportation externalities are desirable and how far the government is willing to go to advance them, even if some of them are in conflict. Certainly, the defense needs of the nation, environmental protection, energy efficiency, cost-effective and reliable freight service for economic development, reliable import-export and land-bridge transportation, subsidized service to outlying communities, and the revenue-adequacy and economic efficiency of public and private carriers alike should be guaranteed on a long-term basis, so that carriers and governments can plan effectively and invest funds with some hope of return.

This statute should not explicitly embrace nationalization, quasi-nationalization, or exclusive reliance on private owner-ship of transportation carriers, even though Weaver points out that "market-oriented policies generally will be superior in the United States given the political constraints against successful operation of accelerationist policies."[11] Options would thereby be kept open for policymakers to react to unforeseen conditions with whatever public policies on transportation organization seemed best at the time. Also, the government should not tie itself to the subsidy or promotion of any specific mode of transportation, including railroads, since it is impossible to anticipate what changes technology might bring to the trans-portation political economy. A good policy should commit itself to supporting all viable modes of transport in their appropriate roles equally, letting profits work where practical and subsidies cover only revenue shortfalls for needed services. Special assistance should be provided infant transportation modes only until they are launched and subject to a fair test of the marketplace and public policy evaluation.

Finally, such a policy should commit the government to collect user fees from all direct beneficiaries of federal transpor-tation development and operations. This should be done equitably by taking from all a fixed proportion of costs and funding the remainder from general revenues, taking into account the proportion of general benefit to nonusers.

Specific recommendations for these and other policies were developed in the 1979 National Transportation Policy Study Commission Final Report.[12] While it ought to be dusted off and studied closely by policymakers and analysts alike, it has aged sufficiently to be obsolete. Also, the report does not specify a large enough government role in transportation as the basis for a new comprehensive statute. A new study commission composed of policymakers with expertise beyond political service,[13] academics from all relevant fields, transportation operators, representatives of labor organizations, and other experts should be constituted with the specific charge of drafting the statute. Such a commission would initiate the new federal transportation planning process. If it is successful, it should be institutionalized and given the further charge of evaluating national transportation policies on a regular basis and making regular recommendations to Congress for adjustment.

Once a general national transportation policy statute has been enacted, policymakers should begin the process of drafting specific comprehensive statutes of policies and plans for each transportation mode as it fits into the overall policy scheme. This must not commence before the general transportation policy is enacted in order to avoid conflicts with it and to take advantage of its planning facilities. Waiting would help prevent the creation of unnecessary new vested interests that would need to be accommodated as changes are recommended. The waiting period would also allow some support for the overall policy to develop and thereby make it easier to bring existing vested interests on board or at least to neutralize them. Since each mode of transportation is linked to all other modes operationally and through the planning process, new transportation statutes should be linked via congruence with national planning, policy, and transportation institutional reform.

Although specific prescriptions about statutes for each mode of transportation are beyond the scope of this book, a relatively detailed blueprint of the rail statute is not. A critical area for rail transportation reform is the transportation policy-making process itself. As Lowi suggests in his analysis of interest-group dominance of American politics,[14] the policy process is not neutral, allowing multiple interests to participate equally and freely and thereby guaranteeing an outcome of just policy. Instead, each process creates conditions wherein some interests win more often than others. And as Weaver, Herson, Lowi, and virtually every analyst, including noted pluralist Robert Dahl, suggest,[15] the more complicated the process, the more likely it is that well-organized and well-funded groups will use the process to advance their own ends over those of less effective groups.

U.S. transportation policy processes are extremely complicated, have multiple veto points for special interests, and have an inability to generate swift, sustained bursts of "blunt and straightforward" resolution. The process produces policies that cope,[16] thereby resembling American public policy generally. The confused and overlapping jurisdictions of policymakers and institutions must be clarified and made more rational, so they can more quickly respond to planning and policy needs. Thus, what is required most of all is institutional streamlining.

The place to start is with the executive branch, because that is where the most confusion and more ill-advised and/or internally conflicting rail policies have originated recently (although Congress and the courts must shoulder their share of the blame). Since major changes in the relationship of the presidency and Congress (such as the adoption of a parliamentary system) are not forthcoming, a reform prescription is limited to proposals that can be enacted by Congress.

The present noncabinet advisory structure in the White House and the method of presidential appointments to rail agencies are not problems "if independent and expert is an appropriate starting point in framing that process,"[17] that is, if appointees are well chosen and are listened to once confirmed. The Office of Management and Budget, economic advisors, and other experts can advise the executive effectively on rail transportation policy. Also, a careful personnel acquiring process can avoid the undesirable deference to senior management shown by past political appointees to staffs and governing boards of rail policy organizations and independent commissions. It can also avoid direct agency appointments to those boards, which leads inevitably to internal friction, as the U.S. Railway Association and Amtrak boards experienced.[18] Thus, other than an exhortation to appoint people who are committed to overall policy directions, who are competent, and who are not in the debt of any special interest, nothing need be changed here.

The real problems in transportation policy processes seem to lie at the cabinet level. The Department of Transportation is overly complex, has no overall plan or direction, and shares too much authority with other cabinet-level departments. It needs to be reorganized and should be given overall authority to administer the comprehensive rail policy statute even if other cabinet-level agencies object. It also needs to develop better planning resources.

The Department of Transportation ought to be able to override the internal executive-branch decisions of independent regulatory agencies on all matters except substantive findings on disputed cases of market dominance. The department also should have explicit statutory authority to override (or to appeal to designated higher authority) the transportation decisions of the departments of Energy, Commerce, State, Housing and Urban Development, and Defense, and the Postal Service, the U.S. Army Corps of Engineers, and other federal agencies.[19] It should be subservient only to the courts, the president, and Congress on transportation matters.

Largely extraneous functions of the department ought to be farmed out to more appropriate agencies (e.g., the Coast Guard turned over to the Department of Defense) or consolidated internally. Each mode (including highway freight and passenger transportation) ought to have its own "administration" that answers directly to the secretary of transportation and that is charged with the planning and enforcement of all relevant modal policies, from safety to rational usage. If that is accomplished, future executive transportation conflicts (e.g., the dispute(s) between the Department of Transportation, Justice, and the I.C.C. about the Atchison, Topeka, and Santa Fe and the Southern Pacific Transportation Company) ought to be resolved before they start. White House transportation policies would be more consistent if this were accomplished. They would also be substantively more sound if "Wilson was correct when he argued in 1886 for centralized administration as a necessity for modern democracy ... [and] that large delegations of power end up more responsibly administered than small delegations,"[20] as Lowi argued. However, Woodrow Wilson was correct only to the extent that in a democratic system, those delegations are accompanied by a responsive process of holding public servants accountable to both higher executives and ultimately the public.

The congressional transportation policy process needs reform as well. Even though Congress was responsible for the formation of Amtrak and Conrail and passed the Staggers Act, the three most successful rail policy initiatives in recent history, congressional rail policy making suffers from confusing committee jurisdictions and inefficiency. Many of these problems are functions of the American constitutional system of separation of powers, which mandates a bicameral legislature and a potentially adversarial relationship with the executive branch. For that reason, they are virtually insoluble short of constitutional change. Barring that, Congress will continue to experience House-Senate conflicts and dependence upon the executive branch for a good deal of the substantive information on the rail policy issues it needs to legislate. The agencies of the executive branch routinely collect such information from their clients. In cases (such as the sale of Conrail) where the White House advocates one policy and Congress favors another, there is a potential for friction as Congress tries to obtain what the executive branch sometimes maintains is "privileged" information. Congress must expend a lot of effort to get reliable information that often cannot be obtained elsewhere.

Congress can improve its transportation policy-making role if it effectively exercises its powers of the budget, government structuring, and legislation.[21] But, the executive-centered orientation of the political culture (which allows the president to shape legislation and government structure through exercise of presidential authority recognized by the legislature) and the self-imposed complexity of the committee structure hamper Congress in its efforts to do so as much as any constitutional impediments.

Sound congressional reform can take either of two directions. Congress could abolish its specialized committees and create general committees like those found in the British Parliament. Rail transportation issues would go to the next available committee on the rotation, and no other committee could claim concurrent jurisdiction because of substantive coverage on a given issue. This would allow rail policy issues and their externalities to be more easily linked at the key stages of legislative writing and markup. It would also make it more difficult for organized interests to capture key members of the specialized committee structure through participation in the electoral process.[22] The entire Congress would have to be captured to have the same effect. Such a reform direction would have the important disadvantage of dissipating members and staffs with expertise and/or interest in a policy area like rail transportation, thereby making Congress even more dependent on outside sources for legislative information.

For this reason, and because vested interests would make such a radical reform highly controversial and difficult to accomplish, more limited reform should be the goal. In order to cure the problem of overlapping and concurrent congressional committee jurisdiction on rail policy matters, each house should create a Domestic Transportation Committee, with subcommittees for each mode of transportation. Such a committee should be given exclusive transportation policy jurisdiction in order to balance the generalists' and specialists' approaches, to curtail committee competition (and transportation issues having to compete with other committee concerns), and to facilitate congressional transportation planning. While a reform like this would not suddenly repair the defects of the U.S. system of government, it would help Congress to be more effective in the overall national rail policy-making process.

A rail policy planning process is needed also in order to remedy the lack of a rail transportation planning component of U.S. national rail policy. A solution has already been put forth with the advocacy earlier of a new national transportation policy study commission and its establishment as either an independent agency or as part of the revitalized Department of Transportation.

Much more needs to be done. First, we ought to emulate the Swiss and develop a "USRAIL 2000" program analogous to the Swiss Bahn 2000 program, which is designed to create a rail system than can compete with highways in a modern industrial environment. The United States needs to develop its own program (rather than importing the Swiss or other program) because effective rail policies depend upon understanding and applying U.S. culture, transportation habits, geography, political economy and resources. With a USRAIL 2000 program, we can develop a long-range rail system plan that will isolate freight and passenger rail service needs and modal interfaces, determine which are cost effective according to overall national transportation goals, and find ways to implement them in ways Americans will find attractive.

Rail transportation planning requires determining how much

rail policy is to be planned and allocated by government and how much is to be left to the allocation of the market. A long-range policy is important and must cover (1) the extent to which we will embrace public and private rail solutions, (2) which solutions will be embraced, and (3) what criteria will be used. The best transportation planning cannot be effective, however, if funds are not appropriated for research and development, for field-testing new programs, and for permanently implementing programs when appropriate. Thus, part of the prescription for an improved rail policy process is to develop sources of adequate funds for existing and future rail policies. A two-pronged effort is needed. First, rail planners must demonstrate to policymakers the need for predictable, reliable funding for rail research, development, enforcement of environmental and safety regulations, and the field-testing/start-ups of new rail programs. Since these are in the national interest, they would come from the general funds.

Beyond that, we need to create a domestic transportation trust fund, which would incorporate the present Highway Trust Fund, the Airport and Airway Trust Fund, and all of the other user fee and subsidy programs for freight and passenger transportation in the nation. When enacted alongside the following recommendation for provision of way equity between modes, a Domestic Transportation Trust Fund would solve the long-range transportation funding problem. It would collect fair user fees (fuel taxes, licensing fees, mileage fees on federal ways) from direct beneficiaries of federal transportation programs.

Funds from the trust would be dispersed according to rules that are consistent with national transportation planning goals. The trust would also render moot the issue of cross-subsidization (where one mode pays taxes for a competitive mode's subsidy) and determine to what extent each transportation mode would receive subsidies for unprofitable but nationally desirable services. Thereafter, all modes would be automatically eligible for subsidy to bring revenues up to the costs for only those transportation services determined by the national transportation policy planning agency to be in the national interest for that particular mode. Other subsidies would be dispensed with. Any other money-losing service that carriers opt to provide in the hope of eventually turning a profit should be undertaken entirely at the risk of the carrier.

The Transportation Trust Fund must charge sufficient user fees to ensure adequate revenue. Furthermore, it must be mandated to appropriate funds equitably, automatically, and predictably, so that policymakers and carriers alike may plan for the future. Any temporary shortfalls in the fund should be automatically borrowed from general revenues and any surpluses should go to repay these debts. Other surpluses would revert to the general fund after retention of principal and interest for a certain period or go into an interest-bearing emergency fund held by the Treasury and made available only if Congress certified a national transportation emergency. If Congress did its part by ensuring adequate seed funds for initiation of the program, future rail policy funding would be self-sustaining.

In addition to these transportation policy structure and process reforms, there is a need for substantive rail transportation policy reforms. Chief among these is the enactment of a national transportation equity statute. It should be comprehensive enough to prohibit any discriminatory treatment of transportation modes or providers in common carrier domestic service. Subsidy equity (including provision of ways), equal labor protection,[23] levels of federal and other taxation, and incentives for investment should be included. This "civil rights for transportation providers" would do the same thing for the national interest as the 1964 Civil Rights Act did: put the weight of public policy against discrimination and destroy the privileges of a favored few to use their power to the detriment of others. According to American cultural standards and classical liberal notions of justice, that is a proper role of government. It is also consistent with the political theory of public utilities.

Another appropriate substantive public policy change is to continue the regulatory reform movement through a national statute defining the nature and extent of national transportation regulation. The statute would declare the policy of the nation to be loose economic regulation of rail and other transportation via primary reliance on the market, backstopped by regulatory authority to set outer limits on carrier and shipper behavior in price-setting, service provision, and service demands. Partial economic deregulation has worked; it only remains to be defined for the long haul and consistently applied to all areas of transportation.

National regulatory policies in noneconomic areas need to be carefully defined and applied in this statute. A lightly enhanced market does not effectively protect the public interest in areas of environmental impact, antitrust, economies of scale, competition, and social services. Consequently, heavier levels of regulation in those areas must be defined and implemented for the protection of all concerned. Strict environmental controls, social service mandates, and definitions of competition and monopoly need to be enacted and funded under careful guidelines of access to the Domestic Transportation Trust Fund.

National regulatory policy toward the creation of transcontinental integrated transportation firms should be clarified. The analogous Canadian experience should be taken into account. Canada is a large nation with diverse transportation needs, and its experience with both transcontinental railroads and integrated transportation firms has been positive.[24] The reasons for the original policy of the United States to give incentives for the construction of a transcontinental railroad in the Civil War period to hold California in the Union (and similar policies in Canada to hold British Columbia, and in Australia and in Bismark-era Germany[25]) are still valid. The United States did not get one or more transcontinental railroads, instead of a system allowing transcontinental interchange and rate splitting between regional carriers, primarily because of the power of existing carriers to block them through their political clients. Though communications and coordination techniques for a national system were inadequate in 1869, they are available now. The economies of scale that would result from a policy of permitting or even encouraging transcontinental end-to-end mergers would be in the public interest. The dis-economies of bigness and the suppression of competition that might result could be defined and monitored. If they became significant costs in the future, they would be dealt with by "backstop" regulation that would not kill the entire policy.

The same holds true for policies that foster integrated transportation firms. If it makes sense for the nation to apply criteria of efficiency and appropriateness for transportation provision by mode, it also makes sense for transportation firms to have many modes to choose from at their disposal in fulfilling customer needs in a way that complies with public statutes and policies and enhances the corporate bottom line. Pursuit of this goal should not signal the abandonment of antitrust protection. Appropriate mandates for competition (whether between private firms or between quasi-public and private firms) should be integrated into these and other U.S. transportation public policies.

The benefits to the public interest of integrated transportation firms outweigh the risks. Benefits include not only domestic transportation efficiency but also enhanced conditions for national industrial competitiveness and energy efficiency. Thus, they should be a prominent component of the comprehensive regulatory statute.

Even if competition eventually is judged to be lacking after the passage of this statute, it could be restored to rail freight services if necessary by adoption of the Canadian model of public and private competition. This would result in federal formation of a quasi-nationalized competitor (another Conrail) with trust fund resources to compete with existing private systems on a broad front. Such a contingency would also obviate the need for future bailouts if major systems went bankrupt.

In passenger carriage, an analogous but opposite course of action should be pursued. Amtrak should be encouraged to expand service modes (perhaps merging with a national bus company or a series of regional commuter airlines), and private passenger common carriers in competition with Amtrak should be encouraged and given incentives to compete with the quasi-nationalized, integrated, transcontinental passenger-hauling system. Both public and private integrated passenger systems could provide enough speed and service variety to be potentially profitable.

Prescriptions: A Moderate Approach

The prescriptions presented so far are consistent with the incremental, nondirect style of American public policy. Together they might be sufficient to continue the momentum of the present rail era in the near future. This is especially true if present policies and conditions are not reversed, for example, the enactment of any of the current attempts on the congressional agenda to reverse Staggers (like H.R. 1393, which was favorably reported in 1988 out of the House Commerce Committee Subcommittee of Transportation, Tourism, and Hazardous Materials, although it never went further[26]), and any more major economic downturns like the "Black Monday" stock market crash of October 19, 1987.

A few sweeping policy changes have plausibility in the U.S. political economy. Though they go beyond mere continuation of the status quo, they fall far short of European-style nationalization or other draconian measure for rail rationalization. Like quasi-nationalization, they are both efficient and consistent with the traditions of the U.S. political economy. Though relatively sweeping, they have ample precedent within the traditions and practices of the political economy. Being nonradical, and therefore possible to enact, their adoption alongside the more nondirect policies would constitute good protection against unanticipated regulatory or economic changes. Collectively, these policies form a sufficient public policy framework to restore long-term health to the transportation infrastructure of U.S. political economy.

One component of this framework that has precedent and should be at least partially adopted is the highway model. It will be recalled that federal transportation policy evolved with federal and local governments developing, building, and maintaining the highway system of the nation. The national government currently allows all who meet traffic standards and pay direct or indirect user fees (with varying degrees of subsidy involved) to use these public ways for pleasure or profit.

It is probably too radical a departure to ask that the entire railway infrastructure be federalized in this manner. But adoption of the highway model as a limited public policy applicable to certain circumstances has merit. According to Ingles,[27] the current movement toward Class I spin-offs of marginal lines to regional and short-line carriers has run into financial trouble, raising the spectre of another round of rail bankruptcies that might threaten vital rail services. As a way of dealing with the troubles of these short lines and other (non-

Class I) marginal rail properties, national policymakers could develop a plan to purchase failing or dormant short and regional rail rights of way at salvage value, rehabilitate them where necessary, and maintain them as federal rail highways. The carriers involved would be free to dispose of their rolling stock and non-real properties at market value. Analogous to existing federal highways in competition with state highways, these national rail highways could then be opened on a toll basis to all rail freight and passenger operators who meet reasonable usage requirements. This would ensure competition on these roads by Class I rail firms and allow many firms to enter the rail transportation business without incurring prohibitive start-up costs that might never be recouped through operating revenues. It would also serve as a way of dealing with future bankruptcies that would cost the national treasury far less than either nationalization or abandonment and provision of alternative service. The only caveat would be to limit this program to only those lines that are not being operated profitably by existing firms and that have sufficient actual or potential business to warrant their being maintained at public expense.

A logical amplification of this program is to develop either new dedicated corridors or to convert existing and redundant freight rights of way from the rail highway program into high-speed passenger-only corridors in appropriate intercity markets. These would be opened on an equitable basis to all operators (Amtrak, state agencies, and private firms) who wish to compete for the business available. If such a program were adopted, policymakers would have another tool to pursue the externalities of rational transportation usage.

A third extension of such a program would be held in reserve for a rail collapse on the scale of the Penn-Central bankruptcy. Anticipating the failure of any vital Class I rail carriers or rail components of integrated transportation firms (and provided that vital services cannot be integrated fully into existing carrier networks), the government would enact standby authority to transform the affected properties into a public rail highway. That is, a railroad would be added to the federal rail highway inventory on the same basis as the failed short lines. Over the long haul, existing and new users would be able to garner profits once they were relieved of the massive capital requirements of right-of-way ownership. The federal government would eventually recoup most, if not all, of its start-up costs and even a good share of its continuing costs through user fees. This federal rail highway could be operated directly by the federal government or "contracted out" in a privatization process.[28]

If the highway model is not followed, an alternative solution to these problems exists, one that is somewhat more drastic in impact even though it has precedents within the North American political economy. Already mentioned in the context of restoring competition, the alternative involves "re-Conrailization" of failing parts of the U.S. rail industry through a program of quasi-nationalization based upon Canadian and U.S. experiences. These precedents (CN, Conrail, and Amtrak in competition with other railroads, airlines, and bus companies) might make this alternative politically palatable to future policymakers facing another Penn-Central or a series of smaller collapses. It would, however, foster less competition and cost more money than the adoption of the highway model. Therefore, it should be pursued only if the rail highway program cannot be enacted. On the other hand, its Conrail-like potential for a profitable operation and subsequent payback of public investment should not be discounted.

Re-quasi-nationalization is likely to be as successful or more so than the original rail quasi-nationalizations only if it is mandated together with effective congressional oversight. As George Guess has shown, conflict between services and profitability within the National Railroad Passenger Corporation represented two different clusters of values of the U.S. political culture. Where the two can be forced to compete internally through congressional exercising of "oversight by tightening fiscal controls and increasing managerial discretion,... [it] permits direction of institutional resources toward improving policy performance ... [hence] an optimal policy will be the product of advocacy, conflict, and competition between service and profitability interests."[29] Guess concludes that "predominance of either service or profitability leads to policy ineffectiveness since waste and service elimination respectively would be the result. An appropriate mix ... works toward the increased attainment of both outputs.[30]

Guess's analysis of Amtrak and its potential application to future quasi-nationalizations dovetail with those of Musolf, Weaver, and this analyst. Any statutes creating future rail quasi-nationalized firms should make certain that both strict congressional fiscal oversight and managerial freedom are sufficiently emphasized within the structure of a quasi-public railroad to give each the base to oppose the other internally.

Another major aspect of any re-quasi-nationalization program would be a permanent budgetary commitment to a public rail passenger system of adequate size and scope. Since the public interests of the nation include an extensive rail passenger system, and since rail passenger service currently loses money (and might always on a stand-alone basis), policymakers should adopt the political theory of public utilities as a justification for Amtrak. Amtrak should be run like a local fire department; whatever is necessary to provide adequate service should be spent as efficiently as possible. Unlike a fire department, Amtrak collects a substantial part of its needed revenues in user fees. If it is going to stand alone, Amtrak needs to be adequately funded for the long haul (probably from the transportation trust fund), and it needs to be expanded to encompass at least all short and medium haul dense-service corridors and necessary feeder lines. Also, the quasi-nationalized organizational pattern that has emerged in the National Rail Passenger Corporation should be codified in an amendment ot the Rail Passenger Service Act and extended whenever possible.

Beyond running a larger Amtrak, a linked but more important component of a re-quasi-nationalization policy would involve the federal government easing its way back into the rail freight business. Uncle Sam should once again become a direct operator of railroad(s) or at least a significant equity-holder in private lines, since leverage and control follow equity in a free-enterprise political economy. As Walsh and Musolf describe in detail,[31] such a practice is common in the United States political economy outside of the rail sector. Both analysts (along with Weaver) cite data that public corporations can be profitable and efficient tools at the disposal of policymakers who wish to do what private firms will not do or who wish to advance other agendas like industrial adjustment.[32] In addition, quasi-nationalized railroads would be effective competitors for privately owned railroads and thus serve as tools of overall efficiency and regulation for a mixed rail political economy.

The easiest way for the federal government to ease back into the rail freight business is to purchase sufficient stock in existing Class I railroad corporations to elect public members of the boards of directors. These public members, carefully chosen for their competency and commitment to public interest transportation policies, could serve as a significant public voice within the railroad industry. In order for this program to succeed, the national government need not purchase a controlling interest in any railroad or a minority position in all of them. Uncle Sam could buy a majority interest in one major freight trunk line in the eastern and western regions of the nation. Or the government could acquire a strong majority interest in one major eastern line (perhaps Conrail, because its stock is undervalued and the precedent is there) and then promulgate an end-to-end merger or purchase of a major western line, thereby forming a partially quasi-nationalized transcontinental railroad. This would probably touch off a defensive merger movement that would result in three or four transcontinental systems, with the government exercising important direct leverage in one and indirect leverage through the market in all of them. A third way would be for Uncle Sam to gain significant minority interest in several railroads in each region, thereby serving as a catalyst for change within the whole industry as other Class I's compete with the partially public railroads and try to match its public interest goals. The last course would be the most nondirect and the least likely to succeed, although it might be the easiest to accomplish initially.

The proceeds the government realized from the 1987 Conrail privatization could be used as seed money to launch this ambitious rail policy program. Given the fact that most of these potential federal properties are profitable, the probability of return on investment from the government-held rail stock justifies expenditures of public funds to finance the remainder of the program. In the long haul, the treasury would be paid back and earn a profit, if future policymakers have the patience and foresight to remain with the policy in spite of short-term ideological and economic fluctuations in public policy.

This analyst believes that the privatization of Conrail will be seen in retrospect by future policy analysts as a mistake, at least in the unconditional form that it took. From the perspective of good public administration, it is generally not sound public policy to sell assets in order to cover current debts. The White House and Congress overlooked that basic business principle. As this analyst interprets the tone of the debate, the primary motivation for pushing the Conrail privatization shifted from ideology to deficit-containment as budget deficits loomed.

It would have been more fundamentally sound fiscal and rail policy for the government to have retained Conrail for another generation. At the time that the federal government sold its 85 percent interest in its quasi-nationalized freight railroad, Conrail was earning about $450 million annually and had already paid back a small portion of its debt. Even assuming a drop in earnings caused by consumption of tax credits from past losses, a softening economy, increasing competition within the transportation market, and failure to reindustrialize its service area, it is a conservative prediction that Conrail would earn at least a quarter of a billion dollars per year after its capital needs were taken into account. Given those figures, the $7 billion government investment in Conrail (minus the amount of that used for labor protection and other external public policy goals) could easily have been paid back within a quarter of a century and perhaps sooner.

That period of time is not too long for a government to wait for a return on its investment even if other policy interests are not served simultaneously. If for no other reason than a desire to get all of its investment back (instead of the $2.6 billion actually realized from the stock sale and government seizures of Conrail's cash before the sale), the government should have held on to Conrail. When its loans were paid back, a gradual and partial privatization (for some of the reasons to be detailed below) might have been good public policy.

Clearly, it is too late to pursue such a policy because Conrail is no longer in public hands. The only way for policymakers to reverse their hasty actions is to reinvest in rail freight quasi-nationalization. However, whether that is done or not, it is not too late to pursue another, closely linked quasi-nationalization policy that makes sense for the public interest as part of a federal strategy for national reindustrialization policy on a permanent, revolving basis.[33] A policy ought to be developed and implemented that would allow the government to intervene in any part of the political economy to prevent private-firm failures that threaten the public interest. Using the successful models of Conrail and Amtrak, the government would invoke quasi-nationalization for whatever length of time and level of investment is necessary to restore health to the firm(s) involved. This would be done according to criteria such as the public interest and restoration of vital firm functions that have failed.

This sort of policy would contain a clear and consistent set of "sunset" criteria. Once long-term health is restored to the firm(s) involved through Conrail-style public investment and good management, the federal government would sell its quasi-nationalized property shares on the open market. It would invest the proceeds in a revolving "bail-out trust fund" to be used to protect the public interest from future critical failures. As a payback for the market risks incurred through public investment, the government would hold on to a small share of the firms involved and would make certain that the reorganization permanently purged the corporation of any incompetent people and questionable policies. The proceeds from the Lockheed and Chrysler bail-out loan repayments to the federal government as well as the proceeds of the Conrail privatization belong to the public and should be earmarked as a source of start-up funds for such a program. If such a program had been in place when Lockheed and Chrysler were in danger of failing, their transition back to health would have been insured, while the risks to the public would have been minimized, since the federal government would have controlled the assets and the boards in the event of failure.

If complete turnaround proves to be elusive as is the case with Amtrak, a separate decision would be made as to whether the outputs of the firm(s) involved are critical enough to the public interest to warrant permanent federal operation, or if sale to other firms or liquidation is a better solution. There should be no presumption that the government would get into business for less than a major protection of the public interest and no presumption that it would stay there unless there were no alternative.

Such a policy and revolving fund are appropriate uses of the public sector in a political economy with traditions like those of the United States. The policy would protect railroads in the near future proportionally more than other firms because of the pivotal place of railroads in the public interest. It generalizes the lessons learned from dealing with failures in the rail political economy to the whole political economy in a manner that makes maximum use of cherished ethics of limited government and private enterprise. At the same time, it is an affirmative policy that does not take an excessively nondirect approach to public policy-making but still contains limits and safeguards against bureaucratic state capitalism. As a public policy it makes government a catalyst for change but not a permanent part of it. Thus, it is a sensible legacy of the Conrail experience. In other words, it should be a temporary but effective rescue tool in case of the failure of a given firm but not a permanent national policy. Thus, it is far different than a general recipe for permanent, pervasive, direct federal presence in the political economy.

A final "sweeping" prescription concerns the future role of employee ownership in the rail political economy of the United States. As Conrail's experience with limited (15 percent) employee ownership and the Chicago and Northwestern Railroad's more extensive experience with it have demonstrated, incentives for increased performance are effective with labor as well as management.[34] Consequently, just as private-industry-style managerial incentives have been adopted in quasi-nationalization in order to enhance its efficiency, employee-ownership incentives should also be adopted.

First pioneered in private industry and given incentives and legal encouragement by federal statute, employee ownership should be made a part of quasi-nationalization through a statute mandating no less than 20 percent employee ownership (in the form of an Employee Stock Ownership Plan) for all government profit-seeking corporations. Drawing upon the Conrail experience, the statute should provide generous incentives up to and including eventual employee replacement of the federal government as the principal equity-holder in future quasi-nationalizations in return for employee agreement to more productive work rules, temporarily lowered wages, productivity agreements, and so on, which are arrived at by collective bargaining. In other words, the second part of the statute should be permissive rather than mandatory by providing a structure of incentives and legal frameworks by which government and organized labor may reach a voluntary accord in the public interest.

A public policy of employee ownership would encourage better employee performance and decreased involuntary federal equity in the corporation(s) involved. It would also provide a qualified, interested customer for eventual privatization. Labor would be served by having a large stake in management. The public would be served by a productive solution that is consistent with the political and economic culture of the nation. All told, a policy of integrating employee ownership into future rail and other quasi-nationalizations is consistent with the present ESOP-enabling statutes and would serve to codify what is already a public policy tendency. It is sweeping only because it gives a legal mandate to a beneficial trend in the rail political economy of the United States and generalizes it to other sectors of the political economy.

Conclusion

American public policy toward its railroads has been inconsistent and even enigmatic at times. Since the first steam locomotive wheel turned on the first wooden rail a century and a half ago, the policymakers of the United States have been trying to come to terms with what to do about this revolutionary way of moving goods and people from place to place. From the beginning they were faced with questions about the proper federal role in promotion and regulation of rail transportation. The structure, traditions, and processes of the ever-evolving government of the United States exposed nineteenth century policymakers to a kaleidoscope of pressures from organized interests. The rail policy goals of the growing nation became intertwined with other policy goals, as the nation alternately promoted and punished, regulated and deregulated its railroads.

The process continues in the present and certainly will not abate in the future. Railroads remain a vital part of the political economy of an industrialized nation. Consequently, the need for a rail public policy remains as important at the close of the twentieth century as it did at the close of the nineteenth century. In spite of the invention of formidable competing transportation technologies and the railroad's fall from grace in the eyes of policymakers, who were simultaneously enthralled with new technologies and angered by railroad entrepreneurs' abuses of their monopoly status, the railroad would not go away. Nor would the need for policymakers to deal with it. Conrail, Amtrak, Staggers, and future rail policy remain agenda items in the rail political economy and the overall national political economy.

The railroad remains a bundle of problems and opportunities for policymakers as the nation proceeds on its journey through its third century. The need for some specific future public policies on railroading has been made clear. What remains to be clarified is a framework for the role of government in the future of the rail political economy and a rationale for it. While it would be foolish to assess the nature of transportation and the role of public policy in railroading and/or its heirs too far into the future, it is vital that contemporary policymakers make such an assessment for the remaining years of this century and the first two decades of the next. Actions taken or not taken now will affect the future just as surely as what has been done in the past, from Jackson to Reagan, affects the present.

One central rail policy question needs to be answered. Formulating an answer to it will allow policymakers to craft solutions to future rail problems according to a rational blueprint. The central question is: How large a role should the federal government play in the future of railroads? If the preceding pages have made any point worth taking seriously, it is that the federal government has *some* role in railroading, even if it is only an indirect one. What remains to be settled is the extent of this role. And if that role is to have legitimacy, the reasons for it need to be clarified. Only a national consensus on solutions will serve as an effective blueprint for policy in the future.

Part of the question is, Who should be helped by national rail policy? Here, the answer is uncontroversial. Public policy must assist all those public and private rail transportation providers who have a vital role to play in the public interest and who need assistance in being all that they can be as common carrier railroads — and no more. There should be no discrimination between big and small railroads or between quasi-nationalized or privately held firms. Nevertheless, the federal government should not be in the business of assisting rail holding company stockholders to acquire real estate or other properties not essential to the business of providing rail service. Rail service rather than the corporate shell needs to be protected. If necessary, nonessential components of these corporations should be separated from the essential ones and ignored as rail components receive public assistance in the form of direct financial aid, regulatory relief, or other rail public policy aids.

Another part of the central question is, When should railroads be helped by public policy? Again, the answer is suggested by past experiences. They ought to be helped before the situation becomes a crisis requiring emergency action. It is far better to employ research and continuous monitoring of railroad conditions according to a clearly defined notion of what shape railroads ought to be in than it is to step in once service and finances have deteriorated to the brink of bankruptcy and abandonment. If solutions on the order of the Staggers Act and its follow-ups are applied while problems are small, the costs of righting things will be much smaller. The window of opportunity presented by early application of federal policy assistance will allow federal policymakers to get the jump on vested interests who stand to profit from weakened railroads. If rail deterioration is prevented before it happens, these vested interests will not grow along with the problem. As long as solutions are consistent with political culture and as long as "governments establish clear goals and then provide incentives to the [rail] enterprise that are consistent with them"[35] there is every expectation that early application of policy will be more cost-effective and successful than crisis management. The best time to address future rail policies is the present.

The last and most important aspect of the central rail policy question is, Why should the federal government help railroads in a free-enterprise system that assumes risks for entrepreneurs? The answer is simple: It is in the public interest. Railroads are vital transportation arteries that cannot be dispensed with in an industrialized nation in the twentieth century. Policymakers in the past have dwelled on the corporate needs (means) of railroading instead of its services (ends). The nation *needs* railroads whether or not they are profitable or costly because they are means toward a flourishing economy and because they can help free-enterprise flourish even if they are in part publicly operated.

There is no need to agonize over the merits of private versus employee owned, quasi-nationalized, or nationalized railroads.[36] Each can work if it is the optimal solution applied at the right time and place. The task facing future rail policymakers is to find the best solutions and make them work for the public interest. Inefficiency, inappropriate policies, and missed opportunities are a form of theft, no matter whether they emanate from public or private railroads or public policy. Because a good railroad system is vital to the political economy of the United States, the nation must have policies that will foster a vigorous rail political economy. Those who have been entrusted with the stewardship of the political economy have an obligation to keep the wheels rolling down the rails to the future, and public policies must keep the track clear and fast.

Notes

Chapter One

1. Oliver Jensen, *The American Heritage History of Railroads in America* (New York: American Heritage, 1981), p. 28.

2. See Matthew Josephson, *The Robber Barons* (New York: Harcourt, Brace and World, 1962) and Albro Martin, *Enterprise Denied* (New York: Columbia University Press, 1971) for two different views on these events.

3. See Lloyd Musolf, *Uncle Sam's Private, Profit-seeking Corporations* (Lexington, MA: D.C. Heath, 1983).

4. See Annmarie Walsh, *The Public's Business* (Cambridge, MA: M.I.T. Press, 1979).

5. See R. Kent Weaver, *The Politics of Industrial Change* (Washington, DC: Brookings Institution, 1985).

6. Musolf, *Uncle Sam's Corporations,* and Weaver, ibid., both discuss these events in detail.

7. See Roy Sampson, Martin Farris, and David Shrock, *Domestic Transportation: Practice, Theory, and Policy,* 5th ed. (Boston, MA: Houghton-Mifflin, 1985).

8. This kind of policy is typical of American public policy according to Lawrence J. Herson, *The Politics of Ideas: Political Theory and Public Policy* (Homewood, IL: Dorsey Press, 1984).

9. William Thoms, "Nationalization, No; Statelization, Yes," *Trains Magazine,* April 1985, pp. 44-48.

10. Richard K. Ross, Jr., "Deregulation and the Freight Industry: How the Carriers are Coping,"*Journal of Accountancy,* Jan. 1986, details some of these changes in the area of deregulation.

11. See Robert Sobel, *The Fallen Colossus* (New York: Weybright and Talley, 1977).

12. See Musolf, *Uncle Sam's Corporations,* ch. 5, for an explanation of Conrail's partly public and partly private status.

13. See Musolf, ibid., ch. 4, and Weaver, *Politics,* ch. 8, for the differences in the evolution of Conrail and of Amtrak.

14. See Thomas G. Moore, "Rail and Trucking Deregulation," in L. Weiss and M. Klass, eds., *Regulatory Reform: What Actually Happened* (Boston, MA: Little, Brown, 1986).

15. *Railroad Coal Rates over the Last Five Years* (1981-1986) (Washington, DC: Association of American Railroads, 1987).

16. This is discussed more thoroughly in chapters 4 and 5. C.U.R.E., Consumers United for Rail Equity, is an interest group petitioning Congress to re-evaluate the deregulatory aspects of the Staggers Act. It has eighty members, almost all coal producers and electric utilities. It is opposed by a railroad-dominated coalition. "House Group Sets October 29 to Consider C.U.R.E. Bill," *On Track*, vol. 1, no. 16 (Sept. 15-30, 1987).

17. All financial figures for Conrail are drawn from the railroad's annual reports, 1977 onward, unless otherwise specified. They are published in Philadelphia by the Consolidated Rail Corporation.

18. All financial figures for Amtrak are drawn from the appropriate annual reports, 1972 onward, unless otherwise specified. They are published in Washington, D.C. by the National Railroad Passenger Corporation.

19. Tom Belden, "Conrail to Reward Workers with Stock Oct. 1," *Akron Beacon Journal*, Sept. 21, 1987, p. C-1.

20. See Garry Brewer and Peter deLeon, *The Foundations of Policy Analysis* (Chicago, IL: Dorsey Press, 1983), especially ch. 2.

21. See Herson, *Politics of Ideas*, for an example of this kind of analysis.

22. See Edmund Phelps, *Political Economy* (New York: W.W. Norton, 1985) for an example of this kind of analysis.

23. See Sampson et al., *Domestic Transportation*, for an example of this kind of analysis.

24. See Sobel, *Fallen Colossus*, and Jensen, *Railroads in America*, for examples of historical analysis of rail public policy.

25. Phelps, *Political Economy*, p. xiii.

26. Ibid.

27. As quoted in ibid., p. xv.

28. Herson, *Politics of Ideas*, p. 7.

29. Stuart Nagel, *Public Policy: Goals, Means, and Methods* (New York: St. Martins Press, 1984), p. 3.

30. Ibid., p. 1.

31. Phelps, *Political Economy*, p. 27.

32. Ibid., pp. 27-30.

Chapter Two

1. Edmund Phelps, *Political Economy* (New York: W.W. Norton, 1985), p. 29.
2. See, for example, William K. Tabb, *The Political Economy of the Black Ghetto* (New York: W.W. Norton, 1970).
3. Karl Marx, especially, used this approach throughout his analyses. Marx and I are both indebted to Aristotle, who used this approach in his works.
4. This is the definition of politics used by David Easton in his influential *A Systems Analysis of Political Life* (New York: Wiley, 1965). It could just as easily be used as a definition of political economy, since it focuses on what allocative institutions do, not what they are.
5. See R. Fowler and J. Orenstein, *Contemporary Issues in Political Theory*, rev. ed. (New York: Praeger, 1985), ch. 1.
6. Harold Lasswell, *Politics: Who Gets What, When, and How* (New York: McGraw-Hill, 1936).
7. Fowler and Orenstein, *Political Theory*, pp. 14-15.
8. Ibid., p. 23.
9. See Mulford Q. Sibley, *Political Ideas and Ideologies* (New York: Harper and Row, 1970).
10. See the interesting discussion of this in Lawrence J. Herson, *The Politics of Ideas* (Homewood, IL: Dorsey, 1984).
11. Ibid, p. 1.
12. Peter Asch and Rosalind Seneca, *Government and the Marketplace* (New York: Dryden Press, 1985), p. 257.
13. See Martin C. Schnitzer, *Contemporary Government and Business Relationships*, 3d ed., (Boston, MA: Houghton-Mifflin, 1987), ch. 10.
14. V. Musselman and E. Hughes, *Introduction to Modern Business* (Englewood Cliffs, NJ: Prentice-Hall, 1981), pp. 5, 15.
15. These goals are developed in another synthesizing work in American political economy: Robert Justus, *Dynamics of American Business* (Englewood Cliffs, NJ: Prentice-Hall, 1982).
16. Ibid., ch. 2.
17. For examples of this, see Lloyd Musolf, *Uncle Sam's Private, Profit-seeking Corporations* (Lexington, MA: Lexington Books, 1983).
18. Ibid, p. ix.
19. Tabb, *Black Ghetto*, p. viii.
20. Carl Friedrich, *Constitutional Government and Democracy*, 4th ed. (Waltham, MA: Blaisdell, 1968) and Murray Edelman, *The Symbolic Uses of Politics* (Urbana: University of Illinois Press, 1964) are the classical analysts of these phenomena.
21. Phelps, *Political Economy*, ch. 10.
22. Schnitzer, *Relationships*, p. 18.

23. J. Galbraith and N. Salinger, *Almost Everyone's Guide to Economics* (Boston, MA: Houghton-Mifflin, 1978), pp. 31-32.

24. Asch and Seneca, *Marketplace,* pp. 79-80.

25. Adam Smith, *The Wealth of Nations,* as alluded to in Herson, *Politics of Ideas,* pp. 40-41.

26. Roy Sampson, Martin Farris, and David Shrock, *Domestic Transportation: Practice, Theory, and Policy,* 5th ed. (Boston, MA: Houghton-Mifflin, 1985), ch. 13-14.

27. Donald Harper, *Transportation in America* (Englewood Cliffs, NJ: Prentice-Hall, 1978), pp. 28-29, is typical.

28. Sibley, *Political Ideas,* especially part 4.

29. Schnitzer, *Relationships,* ch. 6-8.

30. Douglas Needham, *The Economics and Politics of Regulation: A Behavioral Approach* (Boston, MA: Little, Brown, 1983).

31. Michael D. Reagan, *Regulation: The Politics of Policy* (Boston, MA: Little, Brown, 1987).

32. Leonard Weiss, "The Regulatory Reform Movement," in L. Weiss and M. Klass, eds., *Regulatory Reform* (Boston, MA: Little, Brown, 1986).

33. See Musolf, *Uncle Sam's Corporations,* for a general outline of the firms in operation in the United States.

34. Ibid., p. 2.

35. Schnitzer, *Relationships,* p. 16.

36. Musolf, *Uncle Sam's Corporations,* pp. 4 ff.

37. See also Herson, *Politics of Ideas,* ch. 17.

38. Sampson, Farris, and Shrock, *Domestic Transportation,* pp. 398-99.

39. R. Kent Weaver, *The Politics of Industrial Change* (Washington, DC: Brookings Institution, 1985), pp. 113-20.

40. State socialism is opposed to anarchism in this context. The latter wishes to regulate without the state through a decentralized kind of worker control of enterprise. See Sibley, *Political Ideas,* ch. 29, for an overview of this body of thought.

41. Phelps, *Political Economy,* ch. 14.

42. Bertl Walstedt, *State Manufacturing Enterprise in a Mixed Economy: The Turkish Case* (Baltimore, MD: Johns Hopkins Press, 1980) is an example of such a system. There are many others.

43. Richard Pryke, *The Nationalized Industries* (Oxford: Martin Robertson, 1981), pp. 237-66.

44. Ibid.

45. Gordon Smith, *Soviet Politics: Continuity and Contradiction* (New York: St. Martin's Press, 1987).

46. Asch and Seneca, *Marketplace,* pp. 478-79.

47. Kenneth Dolbeare, *American Political Thought* (Monterey, CA: Duxbury Press, 1981), p. 4.

48. Ibid., p. 5.
49. Musolf, *Uncle Sam's Corporations*, p. 6.
50. Dolbeare, *Political Thought*, p. 526.
51. Herson, *Politics of Ideas*, pp. 13-14.
52. Ibid.
53. Louis Hartz, *The Liberal Tradition in America* (New York: Harcourt, Brace, Jovanovich, 1962).
54. Alexis DeTocqueville, *Democracy in America* (New York: Mentor Editions, 1955).
55. Gunnar Myrdal, *An American Dilemma* (New York: Pantheon Books, 1972), 20th anniversary edition, as quoted and paraphrased by Herson, *Politics of Ideas*.
56. Vernon Parrington, *Main Currents in American Thought* (New York: Harcourt, Brace, Jovanovich, 1955) and Daniel Boorstin, *The Americans* (New York: Vintage Books, 1974).
57. Herson, *Politics of Ideas*, pp. 20-25.
58. Eisinger, Dresang, Fowler, Loomis, and Merelman, *American Politics*, 2nd ed. (Boston, MA: Little, Brown, 1982).
59. The complexity of these structures has been detailed in print by Herson, Eisinger et al., Schnitzer, Asch and Seneca, Phelps, and virtually all other reputable analysts of American political economy.
60. See Eisinger et al., *American Politics*, for a broad discussion of these institutional concepts and interactions.
61. See Thomas Hobbes, *Leviathan* (originally published 1651; New York: Crowell-Collier, 1962). See also Max Skidmore, *American Political Thought* (New York: St. Martins Press, 1978), ch. 2.
62. Herson, *Politics of Ideas*, 57-70.
63. See the chapters on democracy in Fowler and Orenstein, *Political Theory*.
64. Dolbeare, *Political Thought*, p. 520.
65. Theodore Lowi, *The End of Liberalism* (New York, Norton, 1969).
66. Dolbeare, *Political Thought*, p. 5.
67. See, for example, the definition in Clinton Rossiter, *Conservatism in America* (New York: Random House, 1955) or in Fowler and Orenstein, *Political Theory*.
68. Herson, *Politics of Ideas*, p. 308.
69. Ibid., 308-9.
70. Ibid., p. 309.
71. Ibid., p. 38.
72. Weaver, *Industrial Change*, p. 268.
73. Herson, *Politics of Ideas*, p. 313.
74. Sampson, Farris, and Shrock, *Domestic Transportation*, p. 5.

75. Ibid., ch. 8.

76. Donald V. Harper, *Transportation in America* (Englewood Cliffs, NJ: Prentice-Hall, 1978), p. xxi.

77. Ibid., p. 3.

78. For a sketch of their abuses, see Matthew Josephson, *The Robber Barons* (New York: Harcourt, Brace, and World, 1934).

79. See the general discussions in Sampson, Farris, and Shrock, *Domestic Transportation,* in Harper, *Transportation,* and in Donald Wood and James Johnson, *Contemporary Transportation,* 2nd ed. (Tulsa, OK: PennWell Pubns., 1983).

80. Sampson, Farris, and Schrock, *Domestic Transportation,* ch. 13.

81. Ibid., p. 4.

82. Harper, *Transportation,* pp. 9-11.

83. John Armstrong, *The Railroad—What It Is, What It Does* (Omaha, NE: Simmons-Boardman, 1978), p. 1.

84. Robert L. Emerson, *Allegheny Passage: An Illustrated History of Blair County* (Woodland Hills, CA: Windsor Pubns., 1984).

85. Jerry Foster and Martin Schmidt, "Rail Terminals and the Urban Environment," *Transportation Journal* (Fall 1975), pp. 21-28.

86. Sampson, Farris, and Shrock, *Domestic Transportation,* pp. 51-52.

87. See the tables throughout *National Transportation Policies Through the Year 2000* (Washington, DC: National Commission on Transportation Policies, 1979) for data on the efficiencies of transportation technologies.

88. Armstrong, *Railroad,* p. 7.

89. Interview with Ohio Senator Robert Boggs, chairman of the Ohio High Speed Rail Commission.

90. Weaver, *Industrial Changes,* pp. 278-81.

Chapter Three

1. Lawrence Herson, *The Politics of Ideas* (Homewood, IL: Dorsey, 1984).

2. Information about these legacies was given in chapter 1.

3. Robert Sobel, *The Fallen Colossus* (New York: Weybright and Talley, 1977), ch. 1, 5.

4. For example, see J. Daughen and P. Binzen, *The Wreck of the Penn Central* (Boston, MA: Little, Brown, 1971) or Richard Saunders, *The Railroad Mergers and the Coming of Conrail* (Westport, CT: Greenwood Press, 1978).

5. Sobel, *Fallen Colossus,* p. 9.

6. Ibid, p. 12.

7. Ibid, pp. 12-13.

8. See R. Kent Weaver, *The Politics of Industrial Change* (Washington, DC: Brookings Institution, 1985), ch. 3.

9. See Matthew Josephson, *The Robber Barons* (New York: Harcourt, Brace, and World, 1934), and Herson, *Politics of Ideas*, ch. 9.

10. Oliver Jensen, *The American Heritage History of Railroads in America* (New York: American Heritage Pub., Bonanza Books, 1981), ch. 6, 15.

11. Herson, *Politics of Ideas*, ch. 10.

12. Michael Reagan, *Regulation: The Politics of Policy* (Boston, MA: Little, Brown, 1987), p. 20.

13. Roy Sampson, Martin Farris, and David Schrock, *Domestic Transportation*, 5th ed. (Boston, MA: Houghton-Mifflin, 1985), pp. 385-94.

14. Martin Albro, *Enterprise Denied* (New York: Columbia Univ. Press, 1971).

15. Ibid.

16. Ibid., p. 361.

17. Sobel, *Fallen Collosus*, p. 119.

18. Since total deregulation of piggybacking, the number of loaded containers and trailers increased by more than 60 percent from 1981 through 1986, according to *Competitive Pressures Discipline Railroad Pricing* (Washington, DC: Assn. of American Railroads, 1987), p. 4.

19. Albro, *Enterprise Denied*, pp. 352-54.

20. Ibid., p. 123.

21. Ibid., p. 126.

22. Jensen, *Railroads in America*, p. 298.

23. Albro, *Enterprise Denied*, p. 363.

24. Weaver, *Industrial Change*, pp. 88-90.

25. Ibid., pp. 98-100.

26. Douglas Needham, *The Economics and Politics of Regulation: A Behavioral Approach* (Boston, MA: Little, Brown, 1983), p. 1.

27. Ibid, pp. 2-3.

28. Robert Crandall, "Twilight of Deregulation," *Brookings Bulletin*, vol. 18 (1982), nos. 3 and 4 (Washington, DC: Brookings Institution).

29. George Wilson, "Regulating and Deregulating Business," in *Annual Editions in Economics: 1985* (Guilford, CT: Dushkin, 1985), p. 58.

30. This thesis is generally argued by both Herson, *Politics of Ideas*, and Weaver, *Industrial Change*.

31. Roger Noll and Bruce Owen, "The Political Economy of Deregulation: An Overview," in R. Noll and B. Owen, eds., *The Political Economy of Deregulation* (Washington, DC: American Enterprise Institute for Public Policy Research, 1983), p. 22.

32. Ibid., pp. 39-41.

33. Ibid., pp. 64-65.

34. 1976 Annual Report, Consolidated Rail Corporation, Philadelphia, PA, 1977.

35. Fred Frailey, "Mountain Railroad Revisited," *Trains Magazine* (Jan. 1985).

36. Jensen, *Railroads in America*, ch. 15.

37. Lloyd Musolf, *Uncle Sam's Private Profit-Seeking Corporations* (Lexington, MA: D.C. Heath, 1983), ch. 5.

38. Ibid.

39. 1981 Annual Report, Consolidated Rail Corporation, Philadelphia, PA, 1982. Perspectives on Conrail's marketing initiatives were also supplied by Prof. John Spychalski, chairman of the Department of Transportation Logistics, Pennsylvania State University, State College, PA.

40. *Washington Post*, March 17, 1985, p. A10.

41. All figures are from appropriate annual reports of the Consolidated Rail Corporation.

42. Douglas Feaver and William Greider, "That Conrail Deal Is a Real Steal," *Cleveland Plain Dealer*, March 3, 1985.

43. Service to West Virginia was abandoned before privatization, thus giving Conrail one less state to serve than in 1976.

44. This and the other statistics about American railroads were taken from relevant corporate annual reports.

45. Stock accumulated in this Employee Stock Ownership Plan was distributed to employees on Oct. 1, 1987. More than two-thirds of it went to furloughed or terminated employees. See Tom Belden, "Conrail to Reward Workers with Stock Oct. 1," *Akron Beacon Journal*, Sept. 21, 1987, p. C 4.

46. Sales for 1987 ($3.247 billion) and 1988 ($3.49 billion) are over this, but are generally declining slowly as the traffic base of the region shrinks and superfluous or lightly used lines are abandoned or sold to short lines.

47. Corporate-supplied organizational chart and interpretational interview with Craig MacQueen, Public Relations, Consolidated Rail Corporation, Philadelphia, PA, 1986.

48. This makes an interesting comparison to the $1.2 billion bid the secretary of transportation accepted from Norfolk Southern for Conrail in 1985. Taking into account cash reserves, surrendered tax benefits, and other complex financial maneuverings, Congress rejected this bid as being far too low, in the opinion of key leaders in the House of Representatives.

49. See Richard Pryke, *The Nationalized Industries* (Oxford: Martin Robertson, 1981), ch. 5, for example.

50. Musolf, *Uncle Sam's Corporations*, ch. 5.

51. Ibid., ch. 1.

52. 1986 Annual Report, National Railroad Passenger Corp., Washington, DC, 1987, p. 32.

53. This label for Amtrak combines terms used by Musolf, *Uncle Sam's Corporations*, ch. 4, and Weaver, *Industrial Change*, ch. 4.

54. Weaver, *Industrial Change*, p. 88.

55. Peter Lynn, *To Hell in a Day Coach* (Philadelphia, PA: Lippincott, 1968), p. 227.

56. Ibid.

57. Weaver, *Industrial Change*, p. 89.

58. Ibid.

59. Lynn, *Day Coach*, p. 246.

60. Ibid., pp. 250-52.

61. Ibid., pp. 239-67. These pages contain quotes and data to back up the generalizations made here.

62. Ibid., pp. 258-61.

63. George Hilton, *AMTRAK: The National Railroad Passenger Corporation* (Washington, DC: American Enterprise Institute for Public Policy Research, 1980), ch. 1.

64. Weaver, *Industrial Change*, p. 90.

65. Musolf, *Uncle Sam's Corporations*, p. 50.

66. Ibid., p. 52.

67. Ibid.

68. Weaver, *Industrial Change*, p. 97.

69. Musolf, *Uncle Sam's Corporations*, p. 57.

70. Kevin McKinney, "A Personal Review," in K. Zimmerman, *AMTRAK At Milepost Ten* (Park Forest, IL: PTJ Publishing, 1981), p. 3.

71. Ibid., pp. 2-5.

72. Zimmerman, *Amtrak*, ch. 5.

73. Weaver, *Industrial Change*, p. 97; *Railroad Facts: 1986* (Washington, DC: Association of American Railroads), p. 61; and 1986 *Annual Report, National Railroad Passenger Corp.*, p. 1.

74. These and other relevant figures are all from the Amtrak's 1988 Annual Report, unless otherwise noted.

75. *Railroad Facts: 1986*, p. 10.

76. Zimmerman, *Amtrak*, p. 74.

77. Leonard Weiss, "Introduction: The Regulatory Reform Movement," in L. Weiss and M. Klass, eds., *Regulatory Reform: What Actually Happened* (Boston, MA: Little, Brown, 1986), p. 1.

78. Thomas G. Moore, "Rail and Trucking Deregulation," in Weiss and Klass, *Regulatory Reform*, p. 14.

79. Ibid., p. 15.

80. Ibid., p. 17.

81. Ibid., p. 18.

82. Weaver, *Industrial Change*, pp. 50-51.

83. Ibid., p. 53.

84. Ibid., and *The Staggers Rail Act* (Washington, DC: Association of American Railroads, 1987), p. 1.

85. Ibid.

86. Moore, *Deregulation,* p. 22, and *Staggers Rail Act.*

87. Moore, *Deregulation,* p. 36.

88. *Staggers Rail Act,* pp. 3-5.

89. Reagan, *Regulation,* pp. 80-81.

90. Ibid., p. 9.

91. William Thoms, "Nationalization, No; Statelization, Yes," *Trains Magazine,* April 1985, pp. 44-48.

92. Ohiorail of Minerva, Ohio, which operates a former New York Central branch purchased from quasi-nationalized Conrail by Ohio is typical of these. I am indebted to Ohiorail President Thomas Barnett for an interview on his railroad's history and public policy interfaces.

Chapter Four

1. Lawrence J. Herson, *The Politics of Ideas* (Homewood, IL: Dorsey, 1984); Kenneth Dolbeare, *American Political Thought* (Belmont, CA: Duxbury, 1981); G. Brewer and P. deLeon, *The Foundations of Policy Analysis* (Chicago, IL: Dorsey, 1983); and Theodore Lowi, *The End of Liberalism* (New York: Norton, 1969) are typical examples of normative political theory applied to policy science. Another useful perspective on this is R. B. Fowler, "Does Political Theory Have A Future" in John Nelson, ed., *What Should Political Theory Be Now?* (Albany, NY: State University of New York Press, 1983). Fowler suggests that good political theory is applied to policy and politics.

2. Edmund Phelps, *Political Economy* (New York: Norton, 1985), John M. Keynes, *The General Theory of Employment, Interest, and Money* (London: Macmillan, 1936); Joseph Stiglitz, *Economics of the Public Sector* (New York: Norton, 1986); and John K. Galbraith, *Almost Everyone's Guide to Economics* (Boston, MA: Houghton-Mifflin, 1978) are typical examples of normative economics applied to policy science. As political theorists do, these scholars use scientific methods or their equivalent to evaluate public policy values.

3. See William Thoms, "Nationalization: No; Statelization, Yes," *Trains Magazine,* April 1985, pp. 44-48, for details on some of these policies.

4. *The Staggers Rail Act: Why It Was Passed — What It Has Accomplished* (Washington, DC: Association of American Railroads, 1987), p. 4, and Thomas G. Moore, "Partial Rail and Trucking Deregulation," in L. Weiss and M. Klass, eds., *Regulatory Reform: What Actually Happened* (Boston, MA: Little, Brown, 1986), p. 26.

5. Herson, *Politics of Ideas.*

6. See R. Fowler and J. Orenstein, *Contemporary Issues in Political Theory,* rev. ed. (New York: Praeger, 1985), ch. 4.

7. Donald V. Harper, *Transportation in America* (Englewood Cliffs, NJ: Prentice-Hall, 1978), pp. 347-48.

8. R. Kent Weaver, *The Politics of Industrial Change* (Washington, DC: Brookings Institution, 1985), pp. 55-56.

9. Harper, *Transportation*, p. 348.

10. Weaver, *Industrial Change*.

11. Roy Sampson, Martin Farris, and David Shrock, *Domestic Transportation: Practice, Theory, and Policy* (Boston, MA: Houghton-Mifflin, 1985), p. 558.

12. All figures in this section were calculated from data contained in Sampson, Farris, and Shrock, ibid., ch. 26.

13. Tax and maintenance figures taken from *Railroad Facts: 1986* (Washington, DC: Association of American Railroads, 1986), pp. 15-16.

14. "The Rusty Spike Award," *On Track,* vol. 1, no. 18 (Oct. 17-31, 1987), p. 2.

15. Moore, "Deregulation," p. 16.

16. *Competitive Pressures Discipline Rail Pricing* (Washington, DC: Association of American Railroads, 1987), p. 1.

17. *Staggers Rail Act,* p. 4.

18. P. Asch and R. Senaca, *Government and the Marketplace* (Chicago, IL: Dryden Press, 1985), p. 205.

19. Ibid., pp. 252-53.

20. Lowi, *End of Liberalism*, ch. 10.

21. See Michael Reagan, *Regulation: The Politics of Policy* (Boston, MA: Little, Brown, 1987), ch. 6, especially, and Stuart Nagel, *Public Policy* (New York: St. Martin's Press, 1984) for general discussions of these issues.

22. The report was entitled *National Transportation Policies Through the Year 2000* (Washington, DC: U.S. Government Printing Office, 1979). It had 527 pages and was amply documented.

23. Andrew Selden, "Sell the Corridor?" in *Trains Magazine,* vol. 47, no. 11 (Sept. 1987), p. 74.

24. Grant McConnell, *Private Power and American Democracy* (New York, Knopf, 1966), p. 368.

25. Annmarie H. Walsh, *The Public's Business* (Cambridge, MA: M.I.T. Press, 1978).

26. *Transportation Facts and Trends,* 12th ed. (Washington, DC: Transportation Association of America, 1976), p. 33.

27. Sampson, Farris, and Shrock, *Domestic Transportation*, p. 436.

28. Harper, *Transportation*, p. 444.

29. Brewer and deLeon, *Foundations*, pp. 17-21.

30. Lowi, *End of Liberalism*, pp. 128-32. Compare this with the British experience detailed in David Banister, and Peter Hall, *Transport and Public Policy Planning* (London: Mansell, 1981).

31. Sampson, Farris, and Shrock, *Domestic Transportation*, p. 449.

32. Lowi, *End of Liberalism*, pp. 130-31.

33. Sampson, Farris, and Shrock, *Domestic Transportation*, ch. 20.

34. John Kneiling was until recently a conservative columnist (and is still an occasional contributor) to *Trains Magazine*. He is a noted rail technical specialist and consultant. Don Phillips, less conservative, was a government-affairs columnist for the same publication, which is widely read by rail managers and rail policymakers, according to interview data. Both journalists have advocated the adoption of the highway model on different occasions.

35. Lloyd Musolf, *Uncle Sam's Private, Profit-Seeking Corporations* (Lexington, MA: D.C. Heath, 1983), and Walsh, *Public's Business*.

36. Weaver, *Industrial Change*, pp. 221-22.

37. "Short Line," *On Track*, vol. 1, no. 18, (Oct. 17-31, 1987), p. 3.

38. "Railroad for the Year 2000," *Marklin New Items: 1987* (Goppingen, F. R. G.: Gebr. Marklin & Cie. GmmbH, 1987), p. 6.

Chapter Five

1. Lawrence J. Herson, *The Politics of Ideas* (Homewood, IL: Dorsey, 1984), p. 314.

2. Stuart Nagel, *Public Policy: Goals, Means, and Methods* (New York: St. Martin's Press, 1984), pp. 423-24.

3. Joseph Stiglitz, *Economics of the Public Sector* (New York: Norton, 1986), p. 14.

4. Even though how that may be accomplished is beyond the scope of this study, it ought to be kept in mind as policies are evaluated.

5. See R. Kent Weaver, *The Politics of Industrial Change* (Washington, DC: Brookings Institution, 1985) for a more thorough analysis of the Canadian rail model, especially ch. 5.

6. "Transportation in Canada," *The Royal Bank Letter*, vol. 66, no. 3 (May/June, 1985), (published by the Royal Bank of Canada, Toronto).

7. Ibid., p. 4.

8. Lloyd Musolf, *Uncle Sam's Private, Profit-seeking Corporations* (Lexington, MA: Lexington Books, 1983).

9. Weaver, *Industrial Change*, p. 88.

10. For a fuller development of this analogous relationship, see R. Fowler and J. Orenstein, *Contemporary Issues in Political Theory*, rev. ed., (New York: Praeger, 1985), chs. 7-8.

11. Weaver, *Industrial Change*, p. 3.

12. *National Transportation Policies Through the Year 2000* (Washington, DC: National Transportation Policy Study Commission, 1979).

13. Weaver, *Industrial Change*, p. 282.
14. Theodore Lowi, *The End of Liberalism* (New York, Norton, 1969), especially pp. 79-84.
15. Robert A. Dahl is the leading proponent of pluralism in the field of political science. His most famous work on the subject (among many) is *Who Governs?* (New Haven, CT: Yale University Press, 1961).
16. Herson, *Ideas*, pp. 311-13.
17. Weaver, *Industrial Change*, p. 282.
18. Ibid., p. 282.
19. Roy Sampson, Martin Farris, and David Shrock, *Domestic Transportation: Practice, Theory, and Policy*, 5th ed. (Boston, MA: Houghton-Mifflin, 1985), pp. 490-91.
20. Lowi, *Liberalism*, pp. 301-2.
21. For an explanation of the "keystone" role that Congress can play, see Morris Fiorina, *Congress; Keystone of the Washington Establishment* (New Haven, CT: Yale University Press, 1977) and M. Dubnick and B. Bardes, *Thinking About Public Policy* (New York: Wiley, 1983), pp. 161-63.
22. See Thomas Mann, *Unsafe at Any Margin: Interpreting Congressional Elections* (Washington, DC: American Enterprise Institute, 1978), especially pp. 106-7.
23. Frank Wilner, "A Watershed for Rail Labor?" in *Trains Magazine*, vol. 48, no. 2 (Dec. 1987), p. 20.
24. See Weaver, *Industrial Change*, chs. 5, 7, 8, esp. pp. 151-52, 182-84.
25. Sampson, Farris, and Shrock, *Domestic Transportation*, p. 4.
26. "Reregulation Bill Clears Subcommittee," in *Rail News Update* (Washington, DC, Association of American Railroads), no. 2485, Nov. 11, 1987, p. 1.
27. J. David Ingles, "Rough Time for Regionals," in *Trains Magazine*, vol. 48, no. 2 (Dec. 1987), p. 3.
28. For a summary of the contemporary possibilities, see E. S. Savas, *Privatization: The Key to Better Government* (Chatham, NJ: Chatham House Pub., 1987).
29. George Guess, "Profitability Guardians and Service Advocates: The Evolution of Amtrak Training," *Public Administration Review* (Washington, DC, American Society for Public Administration), vol. 44, no. 5 (Sept./Oct. 1984), p. 384.
30. Ibid., p. 386.
31. Annmarie Walsh, *The Public's Business* (Cambridge, MA: M.I.T. Press, 1978), and Musolf, *Corporations*.
32. Weaver, *Industrial Change*, analyzes quasi-nationalized railroads as instruments of industrial acceleration and adjustment and finds them potentially consistent with it but not inevitably catalysts thereof.

33. When I first presented some of these ideas for prescriptions on quasi-nationalization at a university colloquium in 1987, they were met with lively debate by Dean William Bittle, a historian, and William Mullins, an urban administrator. The ideas in this section gelled as a result of that debate. I am indebted to both of them.

34. I am indebted to Dr. John Logue of the Northeastern Ohio Center for Employee Ownership, Kent State University, for his perspectives on the uses and effects of employee ownership.

35. Weaver, *Industrial Change,* p. 281.

36. Jeffrey Orenstein, "Ends and Means," *Trains Magazine,* vol. 40, no. 12 (Oct. 1980), p. 74.

Index